Professional Indemnity Insurance Explained

Professional Indemnity Insurance Explained

Frances A. Paterson

© 1995 Frances A. Paterson

Published by RIBA Publications, a division of RIBA Companies Ltd,
Finsbury Mission, Moreland Street, London EC1V 8BB

ISBN 1 85946 008 9

Editor: Alaine Hamilton
Book design and computer page make-up: Penny Mills
Printed and bound by Biddles Ltd, Guildford

Contents

Preface

Many architects will view their professional indemnity insurance policy with as much enthusiasm as they view their last will and testament. However, the need for such a policy has become an unwelcome fact of professional life in the claims-conscious and consumer-orientated 1990s.

The intention of this book is to de-mystify professional indemnity insurance for architects and other construction design professionals. It explains what such policies cover and what they do not, and what the professional person should do to obtain the insurance he needs.

Although the book is addressed to architects, and the examples of typical provisions are taken from policies used mainly for architects' insurance, many of them also cover engineers and surveyors. The principles apply equally to policies for other construction design professionals.

So far as possible, the book records market practice at the time of writing. However, the cover available does change and the architect or other professional person seeking insurance should always check with his insurance broker to find out what is currently on offer. The cover provided by specific insurers is generally not referred to, since such information can quickly become out of date.

My sincere thanks go to a number of people who have talked to me, read the manuscript and given invaluable advice and assistance, in particular Professor Anthony Lavers of Oxford Brookes University, Neil Pepperell, Peter Sharp of Bowring Finpro (insurance brokers) and Stuart White of Hextall Erskine & Co (solicitors).

Frances A. Paterson
September 1995

Glossary

Readers may not be familiar with some of the insurance and legal terminology used. Some non-legal words are used in a particular sense in the book, and a definition is therefore included here.

Aggregate cover:	insurance where the limit of indemnity is the maximum that insurers will pay in respect of all claims arising within the policy period, contrast *each and every cover*
Assured:	same as the insured (commonly used if the insurers are Lloyd's)
Broker:	in this book, an insurance broker, who is a person who acts as an intermediary between insured and insurers
Claim:	an allegation of fault or a demand for money or services
Claims made policy:	a policy which covers claims made during the life of the policy, contrast *an occurrence basis policy*
Circumstances:	in this book, matters which could give rise to a claim
Collateral warranty:	a contract collateral to another contract, such as an architect's appointment or a building contract
Deductible:	same as *excess*
Defence costs and expenses:	in this book, fees incurred in employing solicitors or experts to investigate and defend a claim
Each and every claim cover:	insurance where up to the limit of indemnity is payable for each and every claim arising during the policy period, contrast *aggregate cover*
Endorsement:	a provision of a policy which is in addition to the normal wording and which supplements or modifies its terms
Excess:	an amount, being the first part of the cost of a claim, which the insured has to pay under the terms of the policy

Insured:	the person or persons covered by a policy (who need not necessarily be a party to the policy, although they usually are); in this book, a party to the policy
Insurer:	the party who is liable to pay claims under an insurance policy, and who will be a party to it
Insuring clause:	the clause in the policy wording that sets out the cover afforded by the policy
Latent defects insurance:	material damage insurance taken out by a building owner or occupier to cover his loss
Occurrence basis (or losses occurring) policy:	a policy which covers the consequences of events which occur during the period of insurance
Policyholder:	the insured person
Retroactive cover:	cover for claims made in relation to work done prior to the commencement of the policy
Run-off insurance:	insurance specifically bought to cover claims made at some time in the future, but in connection with work done in the past
Subrogation:	the right of insurers, having paid a claim, to take over the legal right of recovery due to the insured
Underwriters:	firstly, an alternative term for insurers (particularly in the context of Lloyd's); secondly, and in this book, the individuals who consider the acceptability of a risk and determine the terms on which it will be underwritten
Warranty:	in a contract other than one of insurance, a collateral stipulation, the breach of which gives a right to claim damages but not avoid the contract; in a contract of insurance, an unconditional promise by the insured that certain facts are true at the date of the proposal and will remain true throughout the policy period and breach of which entitles insurers to deny liability. Not to be confused with a *collateral warranty*

1 Introduction

Professional indemnity insurance

1.01   You can buy insurance against having twins, against the judge who is hearing your case dying before he has given judgment, or against being abducted by aliens. The number and variety of risks against which private individuals and businesses can insure is vast. Taking out insurance is about spreading risk: a household insurance policyholder shares the risk of his video being taken by an intruder or a tree falling on his roof in a high wind with every other policyholder insured with the same insurer, so that (in the words of the preamble to the Insurance Act 1601) *the losse lightethe rather easilie upon many, than heavilie upon fewe.*

1.02   An architect in private practice will need to consider a number of different kinds of insurance for his business and private needs, for example buildings, contents, motor, employers' liability, public liability and life insurance.

1.03   This book is about a type of insurance of particular importance to a professional person such as an architect: professional indemnity insurance. Under a professional indemnity policy, the architect insures against the risk of being sued for professional negligence – and nowadays the risk of that happening is fairly high. The architect is indemnified by his insurers against damages and costs he becomes legally liable to pay to others arising out of the conduct of his professional business. In general terms, for the architect to be covered, he must have a liability as a professional person undertaking his professional duties. If his liability arises in some other capacity, for example as employer or property owner, then there will be no cover under this policy, although he might be covered by his employers' liability or public liability policies.

1.04   Say that an architect designs an office block for a client, and defects are found in the building resulting from the architect's negligent design. Prima facie the architect is liable for the cost of putting those defects right. If the client successfully claims the cost from the architect, the architect's insurers will indemnify him under his professional indemnity policy. In practice, the insurers may pay the client direct, but their obligation under the policy is to indemnify the architect against his liability. The insured party is the architect, not his client, and the insurance policy is for the benefit of the architect, not the client.

1.05 Professional indemnity insurance is third party as opposed to first party insurance, meaning that the architect is covered in respect of his liability to others rather than receiving a benefit himself. An example of first party insurance is an accident policy, where the insured receives a sum of money if he has an accident, or a latent defects policy (see section 8).

Why buy professional indemnity insurance?

1.06 There are a number of reasons why an architect might buy professional indemnity insurance. Some architects take the view that if they are not wealthy, or put their savings in their spouse's name, then they will not be worth suing. The trouble is that there is no guarantee that the architect will not be sued in any event and if he is, he stands to lose what little he has. A claim may have no merit or be exaggerated, but defending it will cost money, which the architect will have to pay himself if he is not insured. Some might argue that if they have insurance, and if their clients and others who might make claims against them are aware of this, there is an increased danger that they will be sued. There may be an element of truth in this, but this has to be weighed against the risk of an architect being sued anyway, and being on his own without the backing of an insurance company.

1.07 Incorporating as a limited liability company, rather than practising as a partnership, provides a measure of protection against claims. Partners have unlimited personal liability for the debts of the partnership. If judgment is obtained against the partnership and remains unsatisfied, it can be executed against any of the partners who have been sued, and if necessary they can be made personally bankrupt. On the other hand, in the case of a limited liability company, liability is limited to the amount of share capital. The shareholders can not be required to pay any more, even if the company is unable to pay its debts. The directors are employees of the company and as such are not normally liable for its debts. The reason that trading as a company is not a complete protection against personal (and unlimited) liability is that it is possible that an individual employee (whether a director or not) who has himself been negligent, could be sued personally.

SHARING THE RISK

1.08   One reason for taking out professional indemnity insurance
        therefore is that the architect wants to pass to insurers some of the
        risk of loss from claims made against him for professional
        negligence. He will always keep some of the risk, because he will
        have to pay the first part of any loss (the excess), he will have to
        spend time helping insurers investigate and defend the claim, and
        he may incur some costs that he can not recover from insurers.
        However, he can divest himself of a large part of the risk.

CONTRACTUAL REQUIREMENT

1.09   A second reason is that a client may require the architect to confirm
        that he has insurance as a condition of awarding him a job.

1.10   Evidence of insurance is usually given in the form of a letter from
        the architect's broker. As the policy will usually only be for a year,
        the client may ask the architect to send him confirmation that the
        policy has been renewed each year. A requirement to produce
        evidence of insurance may be put in the architect's appointment,
        for example: *As and when it is reasonably requested to do so the
        architect shall produce for inspection documentary evidence that his
        professional indemnity insurance is being maintained.* If the contract
        provides for evidence in a particular form, the architect will want
        to be sure that he can comply. For example, he would not expect
        to send a copy of his policy to his client. If the client insists on
        seeing a copy of the policy itself, the architect would be advised to
        check with his broker before sending it. Some policies prohibit
        such disclosure.

1.11   It is also not uncommon for contracts of engagement and
        collateral warranties to require the architect to keep up his
        insurance for some time. A typical clause would be: *The Firm shall
        maintain professional indemnity insurance in an amount of not less
        than ... pounds for any one occurrence or series of occurrences
        arising out of any one event for a period of ... years from the date of
        practical completion.* In this example, the obligation is unqualified.
        Commonly, however, the obligation is qualified, for example by
        the words *provided that such insurance is available at reasonable
        commercial rates,* meaning that the architect is released from the
        requirement if he finds that insurance is unreasonably expensive

(precisely what the qualification means in practice might be difficult to determine). An alternative is for the obligation to be expressed in terms such as *will use reasonable endeavours to maintain.* The advantage of this from the architect's point of view is that insurance might be available at a reasonable commercial rate but he might not be able to afford to maintain cover. He must however use reasonable endeavours. Not infrequently, the term used is *best endeavours.* This would require the architect to use a greater degree of endeavour, as the wording implies.

1.12   The type of cover to be taken out is often specified, for example *insurance for any one occurrence or series of occurrences* or *for each and every claim* (as opposed to aggregate cover, see paragraphs 3.07–3.09). The amount of cover is usually stipulated, as is the number of years for which the architect must maintain cover, generally six (in the case of a simple contract) or twelve (in the case of a deed).

1.13   A provision similar to the following (which is taken from the standard British Property Federation forms of collateral warranty) might also be found: *The Firm shall immediately inform the Purchaser if such insurance ceases to be available at commercially reasonable rates in order that the Firm and the Purchaser can discuss means of best protecting the respective positions of the Purchaser and the Firm in the absence of such insurance.* Any such discussion might result in the purchaser agreeing to pay part or all of the premium.

1.14   The client will want insurance to remain in place for six or twelve years after the job has finished, but how can he ensure that the architect goes on buying it each year? It is not clear how clauses such as those referred to above can be legally enforced. For example, if the architect does not maintain insurance, it is not clear whether the client could sue the architect for specific performance of his contractual duty. Further, a remedy in damages may be difficult to pursue, since, if the client has no other claim, it is not certain what damages he would recover. If he does have a substantive claim, he can only recover from the architect (because there is no insurance) in any event. Moreover, the damages he would seek for breach of the insurance clause would be the same as the damages in respect of the claim. In either case he is chasing one – uninsured – defendant.

1.15   There seems to be a developing trend for non-standard collateral warranties and terms of appointment to contain numerous clauses relating to insurance. Examples are: (1) *Full and current details of the insurance effected pursuant to this Agreement are appended hereto and the Architect warrants that the premium for the current period of insurance has been duly paid. (2) The Firm will ensure that the insurance does not and will not contain any unusual or unduly onerous conditions, limitations, exclusion or excesses having regard to the prevailing insurance market. (3) The Architect is not aware of any subsisting claim or any circumstances likely to give rise to any claim under such insurance or which might reduce the level of cover.* (The reference to reducing the level of cover is only relevant if there is an aggregate limit of indemnity rather than each and every claim, see paragraphs 3.07–3.09.) Lastly, (4) *The Architect will not by any act deed or default or omission by it or its employees servants or agents allow its insurance to be invalidated or prejudiced in any way.*

1.16   The architect should refer such provisions to his broker for advice. He will also need to consider carefully whether he is prepared to accept them, even if his broker and insurers have no objection. The architect may take the view that his insurance arrangements are a matter for himself and his insurers alone, and try to get the provisions deleted altogether. If he is unsuccessful, he may find that he is able to accept some clauses but not others. For example, taking the last example above, it may be true that he is not aware of any subsisting claims and circumstances at the time the contract is signed, and therefore he may agree to accept that clause. As explained, in practice there may be no effective sanction for breach of such provisions in any event.

COMPULSORY INSURANCE

1.17   A third reason for buying professional indemnity insurance is that it may be required by the architect's professional body. It is compulsory, for example, for members of the Royal Incorporation of Architects in Scotland (RIAS) under its Statement of Professional Conduct. The following provision came into effect in May 1992: *Where a Member undertakes a commission as a principal or chief officer or sole practitioner, that Member is under an obligation, so far as is reasonably practicable, to ensure and maintain that the interests of the client are protected from the consequences of that Member's proven negligence by the holding of adequate professional indemnity insurance or by equivalent indemnity.* Non-compliance could in the last resort result in disciplinary proceedings being taken.

1.18   The insurance must be by means of a policy no less comprehensive than the form of the RIAS Insurance Services Limited Collective Policy. Practices earning fees of £50,000 per annum or less must take out minimum cover of £100,000 on each and every claim. Otherwise, the level of cover must be twice the annual gross fees, subject to a maximum of £1,000,000, for each and every claim. There is a small practice scheme for those with a fee income not exceeding £30,000.

1.19   The Royal Institute of British Architects (RIBA) has discussed the possibility of making similar regulations. The current proposal is that from 1 January 1996 a new Directory of RIBA Registered Practices will be introduced. To enter the Register, a practice would have to be an RIBA Practice (that is at least one principal, partner or director must be a corporate member of the RIBA), and it would have to comply with various other requirements. These include providing evidence that the practice holds the RIBA's recommended level of professional indemnity insurance cover. This would not therefore impose an obligatory or mandatory requirement on RIBA members to carry insurance. However, only insured practices could join the Register, appear in the Directory or be eligible for nomination by the Clients Advisory Service.

1.20   Insurance became compulsory for members of the Royal Institution of Chartered Surveyors in 1986. The minimum cover is £100,000 for practices earning fees of up to £50,000 per annum, £250,000 for those with fees of £50–100,000, and £500,000 for those with fees of over £100,000. The policy wording has to meet certain requirements. It also became compulsory for members of the Incorporated Society of Valuers and Auctioneers in 1992.

Handling your insurance

1.21   In the sections that follow, the cover afforded by a professional indemnity policy, the proposal form, the policy wording, policy extensions and claims are all considered. In the meantime, here are ten recommendations for the architect to help him ensure that he has the insurance he needs:

14

- Use a specialist broker, and seek his advice whenever in doubt.
- Take care in preparing the proposal form, make it look impressive and submit it in good time.
- Think about the work the practice does and the cover it needs.
- When comparing quotations, check what cover is being offered.
- Read the policy documents and if there is anything that is not understood, ask.
- Do not just think about insurance once a year on renewal.
- Never forget the importance of notifying claims and circumstances promptly.
- Ensure that colleagues and staff understand the requirements of the policy, and discuss problems regularly.
- Prior to expiry of the policy, ensure that any matters which should have been notified, have been.
- Cooperate with insurers once a notification has been made.

2 Who is who in insurance

Insurance brokers

2.01 An insurance broker acts as intermediary between insured and insurers. He advises the insured (his client) on his insurance requirements and negotiates with insurers on his client's behalf to obtain insurance. In the context of an architect's professional indemnity insurance his tasks include:

- advising the architect on his insurance needs and the cover available;
- assisting him in completing the proposal form;
- obtaining quotations;
- advising on policy coverage, terms and conditions;
- placing the insurance;
- advising and assisting with any queries arising during the currency of the policy;
- accepting notifications of claims and passing them on to insurers;
- monitoring the progress of claims;
- representing the architect in any dispute between the architect and insurers in connection with claims;
- assisting the architect with any problems that might arise.

2.02 Some brokers offer other services, for example giving advice on non-standard contracts and collateral warranties.

2.03 If an architect has any questions about his insurance – the extent of cover his policy affords him, changes in circumstances, claims, problems that might become claims or anything else – his point of reference is generally his broker. Usually all communications between the architect and insurers will be through the broker.

2.04 The broker's client is the architect and he owes the architect a professional duty to exercise reasonable skill and care. He must carry out his duties in the architect's best interests. He must obtain adequate instructions from the architect, and act promptly; he must also give proper advice prior to the policy coming into force, throughout the currency of the policy and on renewal. The broker usually obtains his remuneration from the insurers, by keeping an agreed percentage of the premium. Typically, for this type of insurance, this will be between 15% and 25%, depending upon the agreement between the broker and the insurers. There is therefore a potential conflict of interests in that the broker's paymaster is not his client but the insurers, with whom he may do a lot of business. Generally, he is acting on the architect's behalf as his agent, although this is not always the case, and sometimes the broker is acting as agent of the insurers (which can give rise to a further conflict of interests).

2.05   Since the broker is usually acting for the insured, an architect could still be guilty of non-disclosure if he told the broker something but the broker did not pass the information on to insurers when he should have done. The broker might himself be negligent in failing to do so (although that is little comfort if the architect finds he has no insurance when he needs it). The architect should put in writing anything that he discusses with his broker and any advice he receives, and follow up any queries he raises.

2.06   Insurance brokers are regulated by the Insurance Brokers (Registration) Act 1977, under which the Insurance Brokers Regulation Council registers both individuals and companies. Only those who are registered may call themselves *insurance brokers* (although non-registered persons may act in connection with insurance, and indeed call themselves *brokers*). All registered insurance brokers have to maintain their own professional indemnity insurance, meet standards of solvency and show that they are fit and proper persons.

2.07   A code of conduct has been drawn up under the Act, and it contains the following three fundamental principles:

• *insurance brokers shall at all times conduct their business with utmost good faith and integrity*

• *insurance brokers shall do everything possible to satisfy the insurance requirements of their clients and shall place the interests of their clients before all other considerations. Subject to these requirements and interests, insurance brokers shall have proper regard for others*

- *statements made by or on behalf of insurance brokers when advertising shall not be misleading or extravagant.*

2.08   The code also gives some specific examples of the application of these principles, and they include the following provisions:

Insurance brokers shall

- *provide advice objectively and independently*
- *on request from their client explain the differences in, and the relative costs of, the principal types of insurance which in the opinion of the insurance broker might suit a client's needs*
- *not withhold from the policyholder any written evidence or documentation relating to the contract of insurance without adequate and justifiable reasons being disclosed in writing and without delay to the policyholder*
- *inform a client of the name of all insurers with whom a contract of insurance is placed*
- *before any work involving a charge is undertaken or an agreement to carry out business is concluded, disclose and identify any amount they propose to charge to the client or policyholder which will be in addition to the premium payable to the insurer*
- *shall have proper regard to the wishes of a policyholder or client who seeks to terminate any agreement with them to carry out business*

Further,

- *any information acquired by an insurance broker from his client shall not be used or disclosed except in the normal course of negotiating, maintaining, or renewing a contract of insurance for that client or unless the consent of the client has been obtained ...*

2.09   The code is guidance as to the professional conduct that may be expected from the broker, meaning that failure to comply may lead to disciplinary proceedings but is not in itself evidence that the broker has been negligent.

2.10   Some insurance, particularly household and motor insurance, is now sold by insurance companies direct to the public. It is not however possible to purchase architects' professional indemnity insurance direct at the present time.

Lloyd's brokers

2.11   Lloyd's brokers are the only brokers who are authorised to place
        insurance at Lloyd's (see paragraph 2.13). This means that if an
        architect uses someone who is not a Lloyd's broker in order to
        obtain a quotation from or to take out insurance with Lloyd's, his
        broker would have to go through someone who is. Lloyd's brokers
        have to meet standards required by Lloyd's and are subject to a
        code of practice.

Agents and intermediaries

2.12   Some insurers use underwriting agents or intermediaries who
        have their authority to write policies on their behalf. One
        example is the Admiral Underwriting Agency Limited who are
        underwriting managers and offer insurance on behalf of a pool of
        insurance companies.

Insurers and underwriters

2.13   Insurers may be a company (such as the household name insurance
        companies) or Lloyd's syndicates (ie groups of individual insurance
        underwriters operating with Lloyd's of London). Insurers at
        Lloyd's are usually referred to as *underwriters* but in this book
        reference is made to *insurers* throughout. (Similarly the
        policyholder under a Lloyd's policy is generally referred to as the
        assured, but the term *insured* is used here throughout.)

2.14   Sometimes, rather than the policy being with one company, the
        policy will be underwritten by a number of different co-insurers or
        underwriters who will each bear a proportion of the insurance risk
        and share the premium. There will therefore be a list of companies
        and underwriters subscribing to the policy jointly. Usually, in this
        case, claims are handled by the first insurer on the list. It is also
        not uncommon to find that the insurance is carried in layers. For
        example, say an architect has a limit of indemnity of £1 million for
        any one claim. If it is a layered policy, there might be one set of
        underwriters for the first £$\frac{1}{2}$ million layer and another set for the
        second £$\frac{1}{2}$ million layer. The insurers on the second layer will
        receive a proportion of the premium but will only be responsible
        for paying a claim if it exceeds the first layer. The lowest layer is

usually called the primary layer and each additional layer is an excess layer. In this case, claims will be handled by the insurers on the primary layer.

2.15 The policy documentation will say who the insurers are. Insurers and brokers should not be confused, in the sense that when the insured takes out his policy he will deal with his broker (who acts on his behalf) and not direct with insurers. However, the insurance policy is a contract between the insured and the insurers, not with the broker (or the underwriting agent or insurance intermediary).

Mutual insurance companies etc

2.16 A mutual insurance company, of the kind discussed here, is an insurance company set up by a group for their own benefit, without any risk capital being provided from outside sources. The owners of the company are also its insureds. The insurance contract or policy is contained in the mutual's rules. The management and administration of the company is usually carried out by managers. The mutual will also generally have a board of directors, composed of representatives from the insureds, which will give direction to the managers.

2.17 At the beginning of each period of insurance (which is generally a year), members pay advance premiums or calls, based on the managers' assessment of how much will be needed to meet claims and expenses (for example the cost of reinsurance) during the policy year. If later there is a shortfall, the mutual may make supplementary calls. The rules may place a limit on how much members can be required to pay by way of supplementary calls. The possibility of members of the mutual being asked to contribute over and above the advance call is one of the main differences between insurance through a mutual and through commercial insurers. On the other hand, while the members are responsible for any losses the mutual makes, any profits belong to the members and may be distributed amongst them. Alternatively profits from one policy year may be used to create a reserve, which can be put towards calls in years with a bad claims record, or when times are hard. The mutual will buy reinsurance, as a protection against large claims. The downside of a mutual is that the members face unlimited liability, in that if premium income (and reinsurance) prove insufficient to meet claims, then additional calls can be made on the members. However, if premium income exceeds claim payments, the balance belongs to the members.

2.18   A number of factors, in particular the level of premiums, availability of cover and claims handling, have led many professional groups (for example, doctors, solicitors, barristers, engineers and surveyors) to set up mutual insurance companies. In 1987 the Wren Insurance Association Limited was set up by a group of sizeable architectural practices. Only those architectural firms who are members of the Wren can obtain insurance from the company, and the members are governed by the Association's rules. The day-to-day management is undertaken by managers employed by the Association and each firm which is a member appoints a director. The members therefore have a measure of control over their insurance arrangements which architects insured with commercial insurers do not have.

2.19   There are a number of other insurance vehicles, some of them used by large professional firms (although not by architects at the present time), for example captives, statutory schemes and master policy schemes.

Loss adjusters

2.20   Loss adjusters are specialists employed to assess, investigate, negotiate and settle claims. They are predominantly employed by insurers, but an adjuster may be engaged by an insured. They are frequently used to assist insurers to deal with claims under household policies such as burglaries and fires. Sometimes they are employed by insurers on professional indemnity claims, rather than having the claims handled in-house or by solicitors.

Reinsurers

2.21   Insurers, both companies and Lloyd's syndicates, themselves insure the risks that they write, through reinsurance. The cost to insurers of buying reinsurance is one factor that determines the general level of premiums. However, the architect need not concern himself with his insurers' reinsurance arrangements since his contract is with insurers.

3 The insurance cover

3.01 This section looks at the basic cover afforded by an architect's professional indemnity insurance policy. As explained, under such a policy insurers agree to indemnify the insured against damages and costs he becomes legally liable to pay arising out of the conduct of his professional business.

3.02 The policy, which is a contract between the insured and insurers, will comprise a number of documents:

- the proposal form (discussed in section 4);

- the policy wording, often a printed document (discussed in section 5);

- the policy schedule;

- any endorsements;

- any other particulars or statements supplied to insurers (thus information given to the broker by the insured and passed to insurers will become part of the contract).

The insurance cover

3.03 The cover afforded by the policy is determined by the wording of the contract documents listed above, and in particular the policy wording. The basic cover will be set out in what is called the *insuring clauses* (see paragraph 5.02). In general terms, insurers will agree to indemnify the insured

- against any sum the insured is legally liable to pay (there must be legal liability not just a moral obligation);

- arising from any claim made during the period of insurance (thus making it a claims made policy, see paragraphs 3.35–3.39);

- by reason of negligence or breach of duty (the wording varies, see paragraph 5.02);

- arising from the conduct of the insured's professional business.

3.04   The policy schedule will specify the name and address of the insured (for example, the architect), the policy period, limit of indemnity, excess, premium, to whom notification of claims should be sent, whether there is cover for optional sections, whether there are any endorsements and matters of that kind. Once the architect accepts a quotation, insurers (or sometimes the broker acting on insurers' behalf) will prepare the policy documentation, including the policy schedule. This will be sent to the architect, and it is important that he checks that it accurately records his instructions and accords with his requirements.

3.05   Endorsements are clauses which amend or supplement the policy wording. Standard endorsements may be printed and bound as part of the policy wording. Endorsements specific to the policy will usually be attached to the schedule. They may be part of the policy when it is first taken out or added during the life of the policy.

The limit of indemnity

3.06   Professional indemnity policies are always subject to a limit of indemnity, that is a maximum amount that insurers will pay in respect of damages, interest and legal costs payable to the claimant. The amount will be stated in the schedule (unless it is a standard sum, when it may be in the policy wording).

EACH AND EVERY CLAIM AND AGGREGATE COVER

3.07   The limit of indemnity may be on an *each and every claim* or an *aggregate* basis. If the former, the limit will apply to each claim notified under the prevailing policy. It is sometimes referred to as *any one claim* or *any claim* cover or as insurance *for any one occurrence or series of occurrences arising out of one event* (in for example the standard forms of warranty). Insurance clauses in contracts of engagement or collateral warranties usually require that the cover be on an each and every claim basis. Aggregate cover is where the limit of indemnity is only available once, in respect of all claims made during the policy period. Each and every claim cover will cost more than aggregate cover, but comparatively little more (say 10–20%).

3.08   For example, suppose an architect who has cover of £100,000 is unlucky enough to have two claims against him in the same policy year and payments are made, one of £50,000 and a second of £90,000. If he has each and every claim cover, insurers will pay both claims in full (subject to the excess, see paragraph 3.13). If, however, he has an aggregate limit he will be underinsured.

3.09   If the limit is for each and every claim, insurers' exposure is unlimited since there is no limit on the number of claims that can be notified under the policy. If the limit is aggregate, insurers' exposure is limited. Insurers may therefore be prepared to offer insurance on an aggregate basis only when they regard the type of business, or the particular insured, as high risk and they wish to limit their possible loss. Insurers may also impose an aggregate limit for certain types of claim (for example claims arising from pollution risks), or under one section of the policy (for example fee recovery cover).

HOW MUCH INSURANCE?

3.10   How much insurance should an architect buy? The limit will apply to any claim (or claims, if the cover is aggregate) made during the policy period, or any claim arising from circumstances likely to give rise to a claim which are notified during the policy period (see paragraph 7.13). Damages might not become payable until some years after the claim is first made or circumstances notified, by which time the amount (for example, the cost of remedial works) could be high in relation to the original building cost. The minimum limit offered is generally £100,000, but this would only be appropriate for a small practice. The recommended minimum is about two and a half times annual gross fees with a minimum of £250,000 for any one claim. It does depend to some extent upon the type of work and size of projects undertaken. Many practices carry no more than £1 million. Only a few practices, even large ones, would carry more than £5 million, but some clients may ask for more, particularly on large jobs.

3.11   It is comparatively inexpensive to obtain a higher limit of indemnity, as there are many more small claims made against architects than large ones. For example, the cost of buying cover of £4 million over and above £1 million would typically be 60% of the premium for the first £1 million layer (in other words, if £1 million cost £10,000, £5 million would cost £16,000).

3.12   If a client makes it a term of appointment that the architect has
        insurance, the amount required will often be stated. If, for a
        particular job, a client requires a limit higher than that normally held
        by the practice, it might be possible to buy the extra cover for that
        job only, and the client might be persuaded to pay the additional
        cost for so long as is required. Since policies are generally only for
        one year, the extra cover will have to be bought each subsequent
        year (although the architect could investigate the possibility of
        obtaining cover for a longer period). In addition, the architect could
        encourage the client to consider taking out latent defects insurance
        (see section 8), although this would not obviate the need for the
        architect to have his own professional indemnity insurance.

The excess

3.13   Under the policy, the insured will be required to bear the first part
        of any claim, and this is called the *excess* or *deductible*, or
        sometimes the *self insured retention*. The amount will be stated in
        the schedule (unless it is a standard sum, when it may be in the
        policy wording). The excess will apply to each and every claim,
        even if the policy limit is aggregate.

3.14   Typically the excess will be about 1% of gross fees, rounded up or
        down to give a figure in thousands, although for a different
        premium different excesses can be negotiated. Insurers will generally
        require a minimum excess, perhaps £1,000 or £2,000. They will also
        apply a maximum (calculated as a percentage of gross fee income),
        since they will be concerned that the architect will be able to afford
        to pay his excess, if the occasion arises. It may be possible for the
        architect to negotiate a maximum amount payable in respect of
        excess in any year, particularly if the excess is high (for example
        there might be an excess of £25,000 for each and every claim, with a
        limit of £100,000 for the policy period). It may also be possible to
        negotiate different excesses for different types of work.

3.15   An each and every limit will be subject to the excess. Therefore, if
        the limit is £100,000 and the excess £10,000, insurers will pay a maxi-
        mum of £90,000 for any claim. In the example in paragraph 3.08, if
        the limit is each and every claim and the excess is £2,000, insurers
        will pay £48,000 on the first claim and £88,000 on the second. On the
        other hand, usually an aggregate limit will apply on top of the excess
        (this is determined by the policy wording). In the example therefore

if the limit is aggregate, insurers will pay £48,000 on the first claim and the balance of the limit, £52,000, on the second. The excess will apply to each claim if there is sufficient cover.

3.16   Different excesses may apply to sections of the policy giving additional cover (eg loss of documents or fee recovery, see paragraphs 6.05 and 6.08).

Defence costs and expenses

3.17   As well as indemnifying the architect against sums that he has to pay the claimant, insurers will pay the cost of investigating and defending a claim, that is, sums paid to solicitors or experts employed by insurers, or incurred with their consent. The claimant's costs and expenses are regarded as part of the claim, and what is being considered here are defence costs and expenses. In architects' professional indemnity policies, defence costs and expenses are generally payable in addition to the limit of indemnity. Sometimes they are included within the limit, particularly for those types of risk for which insurers are only prepared to offer cover on an aggregate basis.

3.18   The excess may or may not apply to defence costs and expenses. It is more usual for it not to apply, in which case insurers pay such costs 'from the bottom up', and the excess will only become payable if monies are paid to the claimant. If, though, the excess does apply, then it will be payable if defence costs are incurred, even if nothing is paid to the claimant. For example, say that proceedings commenced against an architect are settled on the basis that both sides bear their own costs. The defence costs are £9,500 and the architect's excess £5,000. If the excess does not apply, the architect will pay nothing. If the excess does apply, then the architect will pay £5,000 towards the costs, insurers paying the balance of £4,500.

3.19   Although most policies are written on the basis that the excess will not apply, the architect can generally agree that it will, and obtain a reduction in his premium. However, the architect should be aware of the possible downside. If insurers routinely appoint solicitors to investigate notifications of claims and circumstances which might give rise to a claim, the architect will have to pay the legal costs up to his excess even if nothing is paid in damages, or even if the circumstances never lead to a claim.

3.20   Usually the policy wording provides that, if the damages for which the architect is liable exceed the limit of indemnity, only a proportion of the defence costs are payable (the proportion being that which the limit of indemnity bears to the damages). For example, say that an architect has a limit of £1 million but judgment is obtained against him for £2 million, only half the defence costs and expenses will be payable by insurers. A typical clause would read: *If a payment greater than the limit of indemnity is required to be made to dispose of a claim, the Insurer's liability to pay claims expenses shall be limited to such proportion of the claims expenses as the limit of indemnity bears to the total amount required to dispose of the claim.*

3.21   Expenses incurred and time spent by the architect himself in defending a claim are usually not covered by the policy. The cost to a practice of investigating and defending a claim may be high, especially in terms of time. Some expenses might be recoverable as part of legal proceedings, for example costs in relation to reproducing drawings or photocopying documents, or attending court as a witness. Insurers might possibly agree to pay an architect his fares for attending a meeting, for example with solicitors. However, other in-house costs are not generally recoverable even by successful litigants (and this applies to the claimant as well as the architect). Some insurers may give limited cover for the cost of the architect's own time, perhaps for an additional premium.

Who is covered?

3.22   To determine who has the benefit of cover under the policy, it is necessary to look at both the policy schedule and the policy wording. The schedule will set out who is the named insured, and this will usually include all those for whom cover has been requested in the proposal form. The safest course is for every partnership or company for which cover is required to be specifically named in the schedule. Individuals may also be specifically named.

3.23   The policy wording will also have a definition of the *insured.* Included within the definition may for example be any person or firm for whom indemnity has been requested in the proposal form and also any past principals, partners or directors of the firm. Any person who becomes a partner or director during the policy period is

sometimes, but not always, included. The estate, personal representatives or trustee in bankruptcy of any person covered by the policy
may also be included. The definition may be wider and include
predecessors in business of the named insured (ie past practices),
irrespective of whether they are named in the proposal form or not.

3.24   Since the wording of policies varies widely, it is necessary to consider
carefully for whom cover is required at the time the proposal form is
completed. This is considered further in paragraph 4.12.

3.25   The named insured as defined (individuals, partnerships or
companies) will be covered in respect of any liability they have,
which will include their vicarious liability for the acts of employees
and contractual liability for the acts of sub-contractors or sub-
consultants. Some wordings say that the architect is indemnified in
respect of negligence or breach of duty committed *by or on behalf
of the insured.* Other wordings specifically list those for whom the
architect might be liable, including, for example, *any partner,
employee or former employee of the insured, or any specialist sub-
contractor or sub-consultant acting on the insured's behalf and for
whom the insured is responsible.*

3.26   In the context of architectural work, it is virtually unheard of for
an employee of a firm, as opposed to a partner or director, to be
sued personally. However, there have been cases in connection
with surveying work where the employee who undertook a survey
or valuation has been sued. He might be sued alongside his firm or
proceedings might be taken against him alone if the firm has gone
under. Employees, particularly if they undertake work where they
are named (for example where they act personally as planning
supervisor), might therefore wish to obtain confirmation from their
firm that they are covered under the firm's policy if they are sued
personally. The policy wording will usually include a waiver of
insurers' subrogation rights against employees (see paragraph
5.23–5.26). They may also wish to obtain confirmation that their
firm will not require them to pay the excess personally in the event
that a claim results from their negligence.

SELF-EMPLOYED ARCHITECTS

3.27   It is not uncommon for an architectural firm to engage self-
employed architects on short or long term contract. Two questions

arise: is the firm covered for work done by contract workers, and is the self-employed architect himself covered?

3.28   If a practice is using self-employed staff, this should be mentioned to the broker to ensure that it is fully covered. Some policy wordings are wide enough to give cover (for example, the definition of insured may include *any self-employed person engaged by the party or parties named in the Schedule*). In other cases, an extension of cover, set out in an endorsement to the policy, is necessary.

3.29   The self-employed architect himself will need to consider his position. He could be sued personally for mistakes he has made, although how likely this is depends upon the nature of the work he undertakes and whether he could be identified by the claimant as the person who was at fault. (For example, if he does a survey and his name appears on the report he is more vulnerable than if he is one of a team completing working drawings.) However it is better to be safe than sorry and ensure that cover is available in the event that a claim is made. The architect can do this in one of two ways: he can ensure that any practice for whom he works has included him in their policy, or he can take out insurance himself. Preferably, he should also obtain an agreement from the practice that it will indemnify him against losses arising from his breach of duty or negligence, although the indemnity will only be as good as the practice giving it.

3.30   If the self-employed architect relies on insurance taken out by those for whom he works, he should obtain their agreement to continue to maintain insurance for as long as necessary. He should also ensure that the firm agrees not to require him to pay any excess under the policy. There is also a further consideration. If a practice is sued in respect of work done by the self-employed architect, he will want to ensure that he will not be pursued by the practice's insurers, exercising their subrogation rights (see paragraphs 5.23–5.26; any waiver of subrogation rights will invariably only apply to employees, not self-employed persons.) The practice's insurers therefore need to agree to waive their subrogation rights against him. If he has obtained an indemnity from the practice this is unnecessary. The practice's insurers will not be able to go against him, since they step into the shoes of their insured and can only exercise the rights that the practice has.

3.31   The alternative, which may be appropriate, depending upon the work the self-employed architect undertakes, is for him to arrange his own cover (perhaps through a small practice scheme, see paragraphs 3.49–3.51). Although he will have to pay for it, there is the advantage that the cover is under his control.

SUB-CONSULTANTS

3.32   Other consultants on a project working alongside the architect may be employed by the architect's client. Alternatively, they may be employed by the architect himself, in which case they are the architect's sub-consultants. The architect should be clear if he approaches a consultant with a view to engaging him, whether he is doing so on his client's behalf, acting as his agent (when the consultant's employer will be the client) or not (when the consultant's employer will be the architect). By whom the consultant is paid is one factor to be taken into account in determining by whom he is employed, but not the decisive factor.

3.33   An architect is fully liable for the negligence of his sub-consultants, in the same way that a main contractor is liable for the default of his domestic sub-contractors. For example, if an architect employs a structural engineer as his sub-consultant and the engineer is negligent, the architect will be liable even if he himself has done nothing wrong, and there will be no defence to a claim from his client. The architect then has a claim against the engineer, but there will always be the risk that the claim may not be successful, because the sub-consultant is no longer in business, uninsured and not worth suing, or for some other reason. There will also be a cost involved in pursuing the engineer. From a liability point of view therefore, it is preferable for consultants to be employed by the client, rather than the architect.

3.34   Questions about work done by sub-consultants often appear on the proposal form, and to ensure that he has full cover an architect will need to check his insurers' requirements, as they do vary (see paragraphs 4.23–4.25). If the architect employs a sub-consultant, he should make it a requirement of the sub-consultant's contract that he has professional indemnity insurance. It should be made clear that the insurance must cover the sub-consultant's obligations under the contract in question and be maintained for a specified period. The architect should also ask the sub-consultant for evidence that he has insurance, and he will need to check that the insurance is renewed each year. Sometimes it is a condition of the architect's policy that sub-consultants carry a minimum level of professional indemnity insurance.

Claims made

3.35   Professional indemnity policies are written on a *claims made* basis, in contrast to most other types of policy which are written on a *losses occurring* or *occurrence* basis. (This is the case in the United Kingdom; claims made policies are under attack and may not be written in some other European Union member states.) With a claims made policy, the insurers who pay the claim are the ones providing cover when the claim is made or notified. On the other hand, with an occurrence policy the insurers who pay are the ones providing cover at the time of the incident which gives rise to the claim.

3.36   In the case of a claims made policy therefore, the date when the negligence or breach of duty occurred is immaterial (except where a retroactive date applies, see paragraph 3.40). The critical date is the date when the allegation of negligence or breach of duty is made. The insured is covered for claims made against him during the life of the policy only, irrespective of when the error was made or when loss was suffered. Once the policy lapses, so does the cover. Most policies are renewable annually, which means that at the end of the year no further claims can be made under the lapsed policy. This is to insurers' advantage, since at the end of the year they know what claims there are, even if it takes some time to resolve them.

3.37   Looking at how a claims made policy works, say that an architect was engaged on a project in 1989 and carried out the design and administered the building contract over the next three years. In October 1995 his client discovers cracking in the external cladding; he writes alleging that this is the architect's fault and threatens to sue him. The architect should tell his insurers straightaway, and the relevant policy will be the one current when the claim is intimated to the architect, ie in 1995, not the policy current when the work was done and mistake made, say 1989 or 1990. The applicable policy terms will be those of the 1995 policy. Thus, if the architect's policy in 1990 had a limit of indemnity of £500,000 but by 1995 he had increased the limit to £2 million, the increased limit would be available for this claim. On the other hand, if the architect had a policy in 1990 but failed to renew it, he would have no insurance for this claim. For this reason, he needs to continue to have insurance after ceasing practice or retiring (see paragraphs 3.41–3.45).

3.38   With a losses occurring policy on the other hand, the insured is covered for any claims, whenever they are made, which arise out of an incident which occurred during the policy period. It is the occurrence of the event which leads to the claim, not the claim itself, which determines which policy applies. The disadvantage for insurers is that claims could be made under the policy many years after it has lapsed. An example of an occurrence based policy is an employers' liability policy, which covers an employer's liability for his employees for injury or disease arising out of their employment. Say in 1995 an ex-employee is diagnosed as having asbestosis as a result of his contact with asbestos in his workplace, and he makes a claim against his former employer. The employer will look to his insurers, and the applicable policy is that taken out when the damage occurred, which is when the employee was in contact with asbestos. This could be twenty or thirty years ago. If the employer's insurance had been written on a claims made basis, the applicable policy would be that in force when the employee made a claim against the employer. The problems being experienced by Lloyd's are in part due to this kind of long-tail exposure.

3.39   If an architect notifies his insurers of circumstances which might give rise to a claim, any claim that does arise will be dealt with under the policy in force at the time of the notification (see paragraph 7.13). Going back to the example in paragraph 3.37, say in October 1995 when the client contacts the architect he sends him an expert's report which concludes that the fault lies with the engineer. The architect may wisely decide to notify his insurers of the circumstances in any event. Then suppose that in 1999 the engineer, having been sued by the client, in turn brings proceedings against the architect. The architect will have cover for that claim under his 1995 policy.

RETROACTIVE COVER

3.40   Usually the policy wording will afford full retroactive cover, meaning that there will be cover for all claims made, irrespective of when the work was done. Sometimes, however, the cover is restricted to claims made in connection with work done after the commencement of the policy or some other date (called *the retroactive date*). This restriction will appear in the policy wording or, if it is applied to a particular policy, in the policy schedule or an endorsement. Generally, an architect who has been continuously insured will be given full retroactive cover each year, even if he changes insurers. However, an architect who has been in business for a while but is seeking insurance for the first time, might find insurers reluctant to give full retroactive cover or only willing to give it for an additional premium.

FOR HOW LONG?

3.41   As explained, an architect who was principal of his own firm, a partner or director, will need to be sure that he is still insured when he retires or ceases to practise.

3.42   A question frequently asked is for how long should an architect continue to buy insurance? This is not an easy question to answer. Under the law as it presently stands, an architect can be found liable for negligence or breach of duty many years after he stopped work. If he has signed contracts of appointment or collateral warranties as deeds rather than simple contracts, he is exposed to liability in contract for a period of twelve years from when the work was undertaken. In tort, the Latent Damage Act 1986 imposes a long-stop of fifteen years, but it is not an absolute cut-off, and in certain circumstances the architect remains liable even after the fifteen years has expired. Further, the limitation period in relation to personal injury claims is different and potentially even longer. The period is three years but it runs from the date of injury or the time when the injured person has the required knowledge. Moreover the court has discretion to extend the period (Limitation Act 1980). Under the Construction (Design and Management) Regulations 1994, for example, designers or planning supervisors could be liable for even longer than fifteen years. The architect would therefore be advised to continue to arrange insurance for at least fifteen years after retiring or ceasing to practise.

3.43   The cover can either be under a policy taken out by the architect's old firm or under a policy written for the purpose. If his firm remains in business and continues to buy insurance, insurers will generally agree to include retired partners for no additional premium. The architect will however be reliant upon the firm agreeing – and keeping their promise – to buy insurance and renew it annually, and also upon their not doing anything to prejudice cover.

3.44   Alternatively, the architect may buy cover himself, and some
        insurers have arrangements to assist with insurance post-
        retirement, or *run-off insurance*, as it is sometimes called. For
        example, one insurer currently agrees that, provided certain
        conditions are met, cover is provided free of charge. (The practice
        must have been insured with that insurer for a continuous period
        of five years, the architect must have reached normal retirement
        age and his firm must have ceased to practice, meaning that either
        he was a sole practitioner or all the partners retired at the same
        time.) Other insurers have schemes for purchasing run-off cover at
        rates which are reduced by an agreed percentage each year or
        which are subsidised. The architect might also be able to insure
        through a small practice scheme (see paragraphs 3.49–3.51).

3.45   In November 1994, a welcome change in the tax treatment of
        professional indemnity insurance premiums paid by retired
        professionals was announced. Prior to that, retired professionals
        were unable to get any tax relief, but the 1994 budget introduced a
        new relief for post-cessation expenses such as premiums, any
        excess under the policy, and legal and professional fees. The relief
        is restricted to individuals and limited to particular types of loss
        and expenditure which can be seen to relate directly to the
        professional activities that were undertaken before retirement.
        Currently however, the new relief only applies for a period of
        seven years after retirement.

INSURANCE AFTER DEATH

3.46   Unfortunately, the architect's liability does not cease upon death,
        since his liabilities are transferred to his estate. If for example an
        architect against whom proceedings have been commenced dies,
        his personal representatives will become the defendants in his
        place. If he dies before proceedings are commenced, the personal
        representatives can be named as the defendants.

3.47   If there are notified claims or circumstances outstanding at the date
        of death, the personal representatives will therefore need to take
        legal advice on how to proceed. If there is sufficient insurance cover
        available and the excess is set aside, there may be no problem.
        However if there might be uninsured losses, the personal
        representatives may not be able to deal with the estate until after all
        claims have been resolved, even though this could take some time.

3.48   On the other hand, assuming there are no outstanding notifications, once the estate is wound up and distributed, in practice it is unlikely that a claim could be pursued (the sooner this is done, therefore, the better). Thus it would probably be sufficient to maintain insurance until the deceased's affairs have been settled or for a year after death, whichever is longer. However, circumstances vary and it would always be prudent for the personal representatives to obtain legal advice.

Small practice schemes

3.49   There are on the market a number of special schemes for small, part-time or new practices with a low fee income (say less than £15–20,000 per annum, although the criteria vary from scheme to scheme and under the RIAS scheme for example the limit is more than that) or for obtaining run-off cover (appropriate after the architect has ceased to practise, retired or died).

3.50   Under some schemes there is a simplified proposal form, with only a few questions. Assuming the answers are satisfactory (in particular that the architect is not aware of any claims or circumstances which might give rise to a claim) a fixed premium is payable, depending upon the fee income. The policy wording, cover afforded and services offered may be restricted. For example, a limit of indemnity of no more than £100,000 or £250,000 may be available, which may be aggregate rather than each and every claim. The excess may also apply to costs and expenses (see paragraph 3.18). There may be full retroactive cover (see paragraph 3.40), or cover may be restricted, for example, to work done during the policy period and the three years prior to the commencement of the policy.

3.51   At a premium of less than £1,000 a year, and sometimes less than half that, such policies can prove good value, although the architect must recognise the limitations on cover.

4 Obtaining insurance

4.01 This section looks at how the architect goes about obtaining professional indemnity insurance. Firstly, he needs to go to an insurance broker. It is preferable, although not essential, to use one specialising in this type of business, and there are a number of specialist brokers in London and around the country. A non-specialist might himself use a specialist, thus becoming a sub-broker. The architect will communicate with his own broker, and it will be the specialist who is in touch with insurers, which may hinder good communications. If the insurance is placed with Lloyd's, a Lloyd's broker has to be used. Some brokers only obtain quotations from certain insurers and an architect may therefore have to go to more than one broker if he wishes to obtain quotations from different insurers.

Completing the proposal form

4.02 The architect will then need to complete a proposal form. The proposal contains the information the architect seeking insurance (the proposer) will give insurers, and it is on the basis of this information that the underwriters will decide whether they will accept the risk, on what terms and at what premium. Underwriters are trying to get a picture of the practice seeking insurance, so that they can assess the level of risk which they are offering to insure. If the proposer is to be sure that he obtains the cover that he wants, he will need to fill in the proposal form carefully and accurately. It is in his interests to do so, since the information he gives underwriters might reduce his premium as well as possibly increase it. If a proposal form looks ill-prepared, underwriters may take this as an indication of the way the architect approaches his architectural work. It is therefore worthwhile spending time on the form and sending underwriters a well-presented document which creates a good impression.

4.03 The proposer is under a duty to disclose all material facts to insurers. Failure to do so and failure to answer the questions on the form correctly and completely may result in the architect not having cover for a claim against him. A warning such as the following generally appears on the proposal form: *It is your duty to disclose all material facts to Insurers. A material fact is one that is likely to influence an Insurer's judgment and acceptance of your proposal. If your proposal is a renewal, it should also include any change in facts previously advised to Insurers. If you are in any doubt about facts considered material, disclose them. Failure to disclose could prejudice your rights to recover in the event of a claim or allow Insurers to void the policy.*

4.04   The duty of disclosure subsists right up until the time the policy becomes effective. If therefore an architect completes a proposal form at the beginning of March, in good time for renewal of his policy on 1 April, he must be sure to advise insurers of any change in circumstances occurring before the beginning of April. Moreover, if during the life of the policy there is any change in circumstances, the architect must advise his broker and check whether insurers should be told. The duty of disclosure is discussed more fully in paragraphs 4.41–4.49.

4.05   The form should be completed by the principal of the practice, or by a partner or director who has been authorised by his partners or directors to do so (this is sometimes stipulated on the form itself). The broker may assist in completing the form but all the answers or statements are the architect's own responsibility and he must check the details. Copies of all forms submitted should always be kept on file.

4.06   Insurers encourage firms to enclose a copy of their brochure, if they have one, with the proposal form. Details of awards, commendations and matters of that kind can also be sent to insurers together with any other information which presents the practice in a good light (for example, details of CPD programmes).

4.07   There is no standard proposal form for architects' professional indemnity insurance. Each insurer and some brokers have their own forms. An architect might be able to obtain a number of quotations by using one form, but sometimes he will have to complete different ones. The questions on them are similar, and some typical examples are set out below.

4.08   The proposal form will usually be incorporated into the insurance contract either by wording in the proposal form or the policy wording itself. For example, the policy wording might begin: *The Insured having made to Insurers a written proposal on the date stated in the schedule which together with any other related particulars and statements that have been supplied in writing are the basis of the contract...* This is called a basis of contract clause. The insured accepts that the answers on the proposal form constitute the basis of the insurance policy, and the legal result is that the answers become *warranties*. In the context of a contract of insurance (but not other contracts) breach of warranty has the effect of breach of a condition and entitles insurers to avoid the policy, whether or not the warranty is material to the risk or any claim is connected to the subject matter of the warranty. If the wording includes an innocent non-disclosure clause (see paragraphs 7.50–7.53), this might apply and limit insurers' rights.

DETAILS OF THE PRACTICE

4.09   Firstly, the proposer will be asked to provide basic details, such as:

- the name of the practice, ie the name by which the practice is currently known (in the case of a company, the registered name, and in the case of a partnership, the full name, should also be given if these are different);

- the date of commencement of the practice;

- the professional business of the practice (for example architects, surveyors, town planners, interior designers);

- the address(es) of the practice (for branch offices, details of the principal in charge);

- the predecessors of the practice and former principals for which cover is required (in the case of former practices, the date of ceasing business and the reason for cessation);

- the names of the principals, ie sole practitioners, partners or directors (with their age, details of their qualifications and when they were obtained, and how long they have been principals of the practice);

- the staff (both qualified architects and support staff);

- if the practice is part-time, the nature of the principal's other business.

4.10   Further information may be required if the practice has only just set up in business, for example curricula vitae for the principals. In general terms, insurers prefer to insure a long-established firm rather than one that has only just set up in business, because they can then see its track record. On the other hand, if a new practice has only done a few jobs, there is a smaller risk of claims.

4.11 So far as insurers are concerned, it does not make any difference whether the proposer is trading as a partnership or as a limited liability company. However it is vital that the business is correctly described in the proposal form, and any changes during the year are advised to insurers. For example, say that a practice trading as the Angel Architects Partnership obtains insurance, and then forms a company called Angel Architects Partnership Ltd. If insurers are not advised, and a claim is made against the new company, it will not be insured.

PRACTICES AND PRINCIPALS REQUIRING COVER

4.12 The proposal form will ask for details of any former practices or principals for which cover is required. This is an important question, and will need some thought. The proposer will generally want, and insurers will generally agree to give, cover for all past practices, former partners, directors etc, but the range of those for whom cover may be required is wider than that. The following should be given consideration:

- the present practice, which may be a sole practitioner, partnership or company;

- the present partners or directors (and whether they are seeking cover for work done – as partner, director, employee or privately – prior to joining the practice);

- any associated practices, eg those practising from branch offices (do they do business under different names?);

- any predecessor or former practices or practices which have been absorbed;

- any other practices with whom the present principal, partners or directors have been principals in the past;

- former principals, partners or directors (who have left, retired or died);

- the estate and personal representatives of principals otherwise covered;

- future partners or directors (some policy wordings include them but many do not; it may therefore be necessary to advise insurers if further appointments are made during the policy period);

- employees (see paragraph 3.26; some architect's policies specifically cover them, many do not);

- self-employed staff (see paragraphs 3.27–3.31).

4.13   As explained (see paragraphs 3.22–3.23), it is necessary to look at both who is named as the insured in the policy schedule and the definition of the insured in the policy wording to establish who is covered. If in any doubt, the proposer should consult his broker. Care should also be taken at renewal, particularly if insurers change. Any changes during the year should be advised by the architect to his broker, who can if need be tell insurers.

FEES AND NATURE OF WORK

4.14   The proposer will be asked to provide various details of the practice's fee income and the work undertaken. Different proposal forms pose different questions, but set out below are the sort of questions an architect can expect to find.

4.15   First, the proposer will be asked to state the amount of gross fees received by the practice for the last financial year and often for the last five financial years (the date when the financial year expires will also be needed). The figure required is for fees received rather than earned or claimed. In addition, the estimated fees for the current financial year will be requested. The estimated fees for the following year may also be sought. If the firm has been in business for less than a year, the estimated fees for the current year will be sufficient.

4.16   The proposer should check whether fees paid to sub-consultants should be included (see paragraphs 4.23–4.25). Disbursements should generally be included. VAT is usually not included. The proposal form normally makes it clear that fees for UK and overseas commissions should be split. If he is in any doubt the architect should ask, and it is also as well to make it clear what he has included and what he has not.

4.17   The proposer may also be asked to state the total certified building values in the last year, that is the amount certified on the projects on which the practice has received fees.

4.18 The proposer will then be asked to split the gross fees received, usually those for the last financial year, according to various criteria. These may include:

- the work undertaken (for example: feasibility studies, town planning, normal architectural duties, interior design, non-structural refurbishment, landscape architecture, structural surveys and valuations, quantity surveying, engineering);

- the nature of the project, sometimes differentiated between public, ie government or local authority, and private contracts (for example: schools and universities, hospitals and medical, low rise housing both individual and multiple, high rise housing, ecclesiastical, commercial, industrial, recreational);

- the type of client (for example: government or local authority, private, housing associations, contractors, property developers);

- the services undertaken (for example: design, inspection, co-ordination).

4.19 If services are undertaken other than those normally done by an architect (or any other discipline applicable to the proposer) insurers should be advised, whether or not there is a specific question on the proposal form. Examples are project management or planning supervision. If the architect does surveys or valuations (either domestic or commercial) that should be mentioned to the broker, as should acting as an expert witness or arbitrator. These might be regarded as material facts (see paragraphs 4.41–4.42).

4.20 The proposer will generally also be asked to list the five largest commissions on which the practice has worked in the last five or six years, and give details such as the starting date of construction, the practical completion date, the description of the project, contract value and services provided. The practice may also be asked to state the five largest commissions on which it is currently engaged and on which it is expected that construction will begin within the next year, and the five largest commissions on which construction is not expected to begin within the next year.

4.21 The reason that underwriters seek this information is that certain types of work are regarded as higher risk than others, and are therefore rated differently. For example town planning, interior design or landscape architecture may attract a lower premium and surveys, valuations and project management a higher premium than normal architectural services. Providing the information may seem a burden, but it might lead to a reduction in premium. It might be worth setting up a coding system for jobs when they first come into the office, to make it easier to extract the information at a later date.

4.22   Insurers may ask questions highlighting certain types of work that they regard as high risk. High rise buildings, environmental work, projects involving the removal of asbestos, and commissions of an unusual or experimental nature are examples.

SUB-CONSULTANTS

4.23   The architect's liability in relation to work undertaken by sub-consultants is considered in paragraphs 3.32–3.34. The proposal form will generally include questions about consultants or sub-consultants. For example: *When independent or specialist consultants are required for any commission, have you in the past ensured, and will you in the future endeavour to ensure, that such consultants are appointed directly by and paid by your client?* In other words the architect is asked whether he ensures that he does not use sub-consultants. If the answer to this question, both as to the past and the future, is yes, there are no insurance implications.

4.24   However, if the answer to the question is no, and the architect does engage sub-consultants, he will need insurance cover for the work entrusted to them because of his own exposure. The disclosed gross fees should generally include all fees paid to sub-consultants. Some insurers ask that the amount be separately identified because the premium on those fees will be at a lower rate than that for work carried out by the architect himself, say 25% of the usual rate. This reflects the fact that if insurers pay a claim they may be able to recover from the sub-consultants (or their insurers), exercising their subrogation rights (see paragraphs 5.23–5.26). As well as identifying the fees paid to sub-consultants, the architect may be asked to specify the services performed by them, confirm that they have insurance and give their renewal date.

4.25   The proposal form might ask about work put out to sub-contractors (rather than sub-consultants). Whether or not there is a question on the form, if the practice sub-contracts its own work (to other practices or self-employed individuals), this should be discussed with the broker and if necessary mentioned to insurers to ensure that the necessary cover is obtained. (See paragraphs 3.27–3.31 regarding cover for self-employed architects.)

WORK UNDERTAKEN ON PROJECTS ABROAD

4.26   Insurers will ask about work done on projects outside the United Kingdom. For example, they might ask whether any commissions have ever been undertaken where the end product will be used or constructed outside the United Kingdom, whether work is done from offices outside the United Kingdom or whether the practice submits to any other jurisdiction. Underwriters will want to know whether the practice might be sued in a foreign jurisdiction, or be subject to a claim under foreign law. If the proposer wants cover for work he has done abroad in the past or is planning to do in the future, underwriters will seek details such as the country concerned, the date the commission was awarded, the type and size of the project, the nature of the services undertaken etc. The cover afforded for work done on projects abroad is discussed in paragraphs 6.25–6.27.

JOINT VENTURES AND CONSORTIA

4.27   Insurers may ask about work undertaken as part of a joint venture or consortium. In most policies such work is expressly excluded from cover, and so (whether details are provided on the proposal form or not) special arrangements will have to be made with insurers before work undertaken as part of such an arrangement is insured. This is considered more fully in paragraphs 6.28–6.32.

OTHER FINANCIAL INTERESTS

4.28   The proposal form will generally ask whether the practice or any principals have, or have had, any connection, association or financial interest in any other firm or organisation (whether it is within the construction industry or not). If the answer is yes, then full details will be requested. Underwriters might be concerned, for example, if one of the principals has a financial interest in a company for whom the practice works. In the event that any principals do have such interest, the practice would be advised to check the exclusions in the policy, to ensure that the required cover is in place, see paragraph 5.41.

4.29   Details of who owns or controls the practice, if it is not the principals, may also be sought and should in any event be disclosed.

QUALITY ASSURANCE

4.30   Proposal forms generally do not include a question asking whether the proposer is quality assured. However, if a practice does have a quality assurance system in place (whether it is certificated or not), this is certainly something that can be mentioned to insurers.

4.31   Some underwriters will give a premium credit to a certificated practice of up to 10%, or reduce the excess. Others do not specifically allow a credit, although it is a factor that they will bear in mind when assessing the premium. Underwriters are likely to be more impressed by a system that has been assessed by an independent third party than one that has not. They may however be concerned that being quality assured could increase the architect's standard of care. A practice should therefore guard against this happening so far as it can, for example by looking carefully at its documentation. Also the policy will cover claims arising out of work done prior to the quality assurance system being in place. If a practice tells insurers that it uses a quality assurance system, it must do so on every job, or advise insurers.

4.32   In any event, if through having a quality assurance system a proposer has a good claims record and can present itself as an efficient and well managed firm, then that is likely to result in insurers regarding them as a good risk, deserving a lower premium.

PREVIOUS INSURANCE RECORD

4.33   The proposal form will include a question about previous insurance held. For example, underwriters might ask for details of the policy held in the previous year, or the last policy held, including the name of the insurers, limit of indemnity, excess, expiry date etc. Alternatively, they might ask for details of insurance held over the past three years. If there has not been continuous insurance cover, insurers might ask why not and might impose special terms (for example, declining to give full retroactive cover, see paragraph 3.40).

4.34   A question similar to the following will also be found:

Has any insurer ever

– declined a proposal or renewal?
– imposed special terms or extra premium?
– cancelled or voided your insurance?

4.35   With regard to special terms, the sort of things that need to be disclosed are the restriction of cover for certain types of work or for specific contracts. If the answer to any of these questions is yes, then underwriters will require full details before they give a quotation. His broker may be able to assist the architect in answering the question, particularly if he was the broker involved at the time when the proposal was declined, or whatever. The proposer may be able to give a perfectly satisfactory answer or he may not, in which case insurers might be reluctant to give cover at all or themselves impose special terms.

CLAIMS RECORD AND CLAIMS DETAILS

4.36   Important questions in the proposal form are those regarding claims. The notes on the RIBA scheme proposal form comment: *Over the years it is this question which has created the most disputes between Insurers and Insureds. It could be regarded as the most important question of all and it would appear to be the main reason why many policies have been avoided or claims rejected by Insurers. This being so all of these questions should be answered by you with care and accuracy. 'See your records', 'Refer to broker' or the like is not acceptable.*

4.37   Details of the firm's past claims record will be sought, in a question such as the following: *Have any claims for professional negligence error or omission (successful or otherwise) been made against the firm, its predecessors in business or its present or past principals, partners or directors?* This question refers to claims only (that is, not circumstances which may give rise to a claim, see paragraph 7.03) but encompasses claims that have been resolved as well as on-going ones. It also refers not only to claims against the present practice but others covered under the policy. Often details of claims made over the last ten years only are requested, but subject to that, every claim should be included. A full explanation of the claim should be given including the date when it was made, the amount claimed, the amount paid and any comments. The easiest thing is if the practice has a list which is updated each year on renewal. As a separate question, the proposer is sometimes asked to list all circumstances (as opposed to claims) notified to insurers, both those accepted by them as notifications and those not accepted.

4.38 The proposer will also be asked whether he is aware of any present or future claims, and a typical question reads: *Are any principals, partners or directors aware, after enquiry, of any circumstances which may give rise to a claim against the firm or its predecessors in business or any of the present or former principals, partners or directors?* What constitutes notifiable *circumstances which may give rise to a claim* is discussed in paragraphs 7.03–7.08. It is important that the proposer does make enquiry of those referred to in the question, and the staff as well, in all offices. *If in doubt reveal rather than conceal*, the architect is advised in one proposal form.

4.39 When answering these questions in particular, the proposer should remember his duty to disclose material facts (see paragraphs 4.41–4.49).

COVER REQUIRED

4.40 The proposer will be asked about the cover required, that is the limit of indemnity, excess and matters of that kind. Quotations for different limits and excesses can be requested.

Duty of disclosure

4.41 An insurance policy is one of a special limited class of contracts which require both parties, the insured and insurers, to exercise the utmost good faith in their dealings with each other. Thus it is called a contract *uberrimae fidei* or *of utmost good faith*. This means that the parties have obligations over and above those they have under other contracts. In particular, a party seeking insurance is under an obligation to disclose all those facts regarded by the law as material which he knows or is presumed to know, that is every fact which, in the ordinary course of business affairs, ought to be known by him. The facts about the risk are known to the insured but not to insurers, and underwriters will want the fullest information about any risk that they insure.

4.42   Material facts are those which would influence a prudent insurer in deciding whether to accept the risk and if so on what terms, as to premium or otherwise. They are not only those facts which would have a decisive influence, that is which would be decisive in determining what prudent insurers would charge or whether they would accept the risk. In the case of *Pan Atlantic Insurance Co Ltd v Pine Top Co Ltd* [1994] 3 WLR 677, the House of Lords decided on a so-called *need to know* test. A fact is material, they said, if an underwriter would like to be aware of the fact, and it is not necessary to show that his decision would have been different had he known of the fact.

4.43   Thus far, the Lords upheld previous decisions. However, they then departed from the law as it had previously been understood. It had been thought that whenever a proposer was guilty of non-disclosure, whatever the nature of the information not disclosed, insurers could avoid the policy. However, the Lords held that insurers can only avoid the policy if the non-disclosure or misrepresentation induced the making of the policy, either at all or on the terms on which it was made. It is necessary to go on to establish the second element of *inducement*. There is therefore an additional hurdle which insurers have to overcome, although how this will operate in practice remains to be seen.

4.44   If the policy is avoided, it means that it becomes null and void as if it had never existed. The parties are put in the position they would be in if there had never been a policy in place. The premium is repayable and there is no cover for any claims notified. If insurers have paid any claims prior to the policy becoming void, they can seek reimbursement from the insured. In practice, they might set the premium off against such payments.

4.45   Some proposal forms include a question specifically asking whether there are any other material facts which ought to be disclosed, but the duty arises whether or not there is such a question on the proposal form. Matters which might increase or alter the risk are material facts. Many are referred to elsewhere in the book as matters which should be brought to insurers' attention. Some further examples are given in the next paragraph, but they are examples only and do not comprise a check list.

4.46 The following are the sort of matters which should be disclosed:

- where the architect, or a colleague, suffers from a physical disability or nervous impediment which is likely to affect the performance of his work, permanently or temporarily;

- where a member of staff has a criminal record or has been dismissed for dishonesty or incompetence;

- where the practice is in serious financial difficulty, for example has agreed a creditors' voluntary arrangement, or an associated practice has gone into liquidation or receivership;

- where the composition of the firm is likely to change, for example the architect is planning to retire, or is intending to incorporate as a company or amalgamate with another practice.

4.47 This duty of utmost good faith is often extended by the wording of the proposal form and policy wording to become not only a common law duty but a contractual obligation as well. For example, at the end of the proposal form, the proposer will be asked to sign a declaration in terms such as the following: *I declare that after enquiry the statements and particulars in this proposal form are true and that I have not mis-stated or suppressed any material facts. I agree that this proposal form, together with any other information supplied by me, shall form the basis of any policy of insurance effected hereon. I undertake to inform Insurers of any material alteration to these facts occurring before completion of the policy of insurance.* The effect of signing this declaration is that the proposer warrants the accuracy of the answers on the proposal form and that he has not withheld or failed to disclose any material facts. The effect of a breach of warranty is discussed in paragraph 4.08.

4.48 As explained, it is only in contracts of insurance (and other contracts of utmost good faith) that the parties have a positive duty to disclose. In other contracts, the law imposes on the parties a duty not to misrepresent the facts. The line between non-disclosure and misrepresentation is often imperceptible and the two are generally talked of together.

4.49 How the harshness of the rules discussed above may be alleviated by the policy wording is explained in paragraphs 7.50–7.53.

The quotation

HOW IS THE PREMIUM CALCULATED?

4.50   The premium will be calculated by the underwriters (either those employed by insurers themselves or by underwriting managers if they are used), or occasionally by the broker under a delegated authority. Every practice seeking insurance will be individually rated, and the underwriters will use their skill and experience to assess the risk from the information they have on the proposal form. The only exception to this is under a small practice scheme, where premiums might be charged as a fixed percentage of fee income or in bands. The underwriters may raise queries with the broker, who may have to refer back to the architect.

4.51   There is no precise formula for calculating the premium for this type of insurance, and all insurers will have their own method. Some factors will decrease the perceived risk and thus reduce the premium. Other factors will result in a premium loading. Sometimes underwriters will be unwilling to quote for the risk at all, since insurers have their own guidelines for the sort of business that they want to write (for example, some may not insure practices who do a lot of commercial valuation work or project management). Alternatively, insurers may be unwilling to take on that particular firm or they may take on the risk but exclude certain work from cover. If this happens, the architect will need his broker's assistance to negotiate with insurers or seek out alternative quotations. Different insurers will be competitive on different types of risk, or for different cover.

4.52   The biggest single factor affecting the premium is the practice's fee income. The proposer will usually be rated on the fees for the last financial year, but premiums may be increased or decreased according to the level of fees in the last three years. For example, if the fees for last year are much lower than those for previous years, the premium may be weighted to take this into account. Conversely, if the practice is comparatively new (or full retroactive cover is not given, see paragraph 3.40) and there is little or no exposure in respect of work done in the past, a discount may be applied.

4.53   The premium will also depend upon such factors as the limit of indemnity, size of the excess (and whether it applies to defence costs and expenses), whether the cover is any one claim or aggregate, the size of the practice, the cover provided (for example whether extensions are included), and the type of work undertaken. The underwriters will then consider all the information they have in order to assess the overall quality of the firm and the likelihood of claims. Examples of other factors which may be taken into account are how long the practice has been in business, the qualifications and experience of the principals, the ratio of fees to the volume of building work certified, the partner/staff ratio and the partner/fees ratio. A decrease in fee income over the early 1990s is to be expected, but a rapid increase in fees might cause underwriters to question the firm's quality control. Different types of work and different clientele may attract different rates.

4.54   An example illustrates how different insurers may view the same risk and why premiums vary. Say that for a limit of indemnity of £1 million in respect of each and every claim, for a good practice with a claims free record, insurers require a rate on fees of 1.5%. The practice declares gross fees for the previous year of £275,000. This gives a premium of £4,125. However, some insurers take the average fee income for the past three years, since for many practices fee income is still declining and the earnings in the current year may not be an accurate indication of the amount of work done in previous years. Say the fees for the previous two years were £395,000 and £344,000, giving an average of £338,000. The same rate of 1.5% would then give a premium of £5,070.

4.55   Last but not least, the practice's claims record will be taken into account when the premium is calculated. If the proposer has never had any claims or no claims resulting in payments, the basic rate will be discounted, up to perhaps 20%. On the other hand, if the proposer has had a number of claims on which payments have been made or are likely to be required, the premium may be loaded. This may apply if defence costs and expenses have been incurred in investigating or defending a claim, even if no damages have been paid to a claimant. Sometimes a higher excess will be required and there might be other conditions or restrictions. For example, new insurers taking on the practice for the first time might exclude a project on which there has been a sizeable claim. In some instances, if underwriters are particularly unhappy about a proposer's claims record, they might decline to offer insurance at all.

4.56   Will notifying claims or circumstances which might lead to a claim increase the premium? The answer is that it might, but not necessarily. When assessing an architect's premium, underwriters need to weigh up the risk, and one indicator is whether claims payments have been made before. If his claims record indicates that the architect is a bad risk, then he can expect to pay increased insurance premiums. Indeed, if it were otherwise architects with a good record would be paying for the mistakes of those with a bad one. On the other hand, an architect who notifies circumstances in good time and works effectively with insurers can make a real contribution to the management of risk, and to keeping his premiums down.

4.57   In any event, the architect must bear in mind the possible down-side if he does not properly notify. He is under an obligation to tell insurers about claims or circumstances likely to give rise to claims, and cover may be prejudiced if this is not done. If there is an indication that the architect does not always notify claims and circumstances when he should, this will be taken into account by underwriters. Further, circumstances may never become claims if dealt with promptly and claims can be mitigated if properly handled. However, if insurers do have to make payments in respect of claims, this will be taken into account when the premium is calculated.

4.58   Market forces are an additional factor in determining the level of premium, as is the cost of reinsurance (that is, the cost to insurers of insuring their exposure). When premiums are low, the market is described as *soft;* when premiums are high, it is described as *hard*. At the present time, the typical cost of insurance for an architect could be between one and five per cent of gross fee income, for a limit of one million pounds for each and every claim. In the early and mid 1990s, premiums for architects have been low and the insurance market competitive. Premiums for surveyors on the other hand have increased considerably over the last few years, reflecting in particular the number and size of claims that have been made against surveyors and valuers as a result of the collapse of the property market in the late 1980s. For engineers the market is also soft, although rates vary considerably depending upon the discipline.

EXCLUSIONS AND LIMITATIONS ON COVER

4.59   As has been explained, underwriters might give a quotation but exclude certain matters from cover. For example, work done by certain named persons, partnerships or companies, or work done from a particular office might be excluded, as might work on a certain named project (perhaps because of bad claims experience).

COMPARING QUOTATIONS

4.60   The broker will send the architect details of the quotation or quotations he has obtained on the architect's behalf. There may be a number of differences between what is offered by different insurers, apart from price. The architect should ensure that he is comparing like with like, and is fully aware of what cover is being given. One quotation may be a few hundred or several thousand pounds cheaper than another, but the saving may be quickly cancelled out if the cover is less. Some examples of the factors that should be considered are set out below. Some matters will be important to one architect, some to another. The list is not exhaustive, since cover requirements vary considerably from one business to another.

- Is the cover on an each and every claim or aggregate basis (see paragraphs 3.07–3.09)?

- What is the limit of indemnity (and are defence costs and expenses payable in addition, see paragraph 3.17)?

- What is the excess, and does it apply to defence costs and expenses or not (see paragraphs 3.13–3.16 and 3.18–3.19)?

- Is there full cover for the work undertaken by the practice and for all those for whom cover is required?

- What cover is there for extensions such as fee recovery or criminal prosecution defence costs (see paragraphs 6.08–6.13 and 6.14–6.17)?

- Does the policy wording cover breach of professional duty or negligence (see paragraphs 5.02–5.04) and is there cover for fitness for purpose obligations or indemnities (see paragraphs 5.09–5.14)?

- What is insurers' attitude to liabilities assumed under collateral warranties, in standard form or non standard (see paragraphs 6.18–6.24)?

- Is there full retroactive cover (see paragraph 3.40)?

- Is there full cover for all the work undertaken by the practice (eg surveys and valuations, project management, planning supervision)?

- Does the policy wording include any conditions or exclusions which mean that the requirements of the business are not met?

- Are there any non-standard exclusions imposed by insurers (eg claims on a particular project)?

- Is there a facility for paying the premium by instalments?

- On renewal, will the insurers be the same as last year, or will there be a change of insurers (see paragraphs 4.66–4.71)?

- Are any services offered (eg advice on warranties, a subsidised legal service or risk management)?

- Are any extras offered (eg cover during maternity leave or after retirement)?

- Does the wording include an innocent non-disclosure clause (see paragraphs 7.50–7.53)?

- How are claims handled (see paragraph 7.24)?

4.61   It is part of the broker's job to advise the architect and help him reach a decision, so if the architect needs any assistance he should seek it. It may be possible to negotiate the addition of cover not otherwise offered.

4.62   Since October 1994, insurers have been required to charge insurance premium tax, currently $2\frac{1}{2}\%$, which is payable in addition to the premium.

Renewal

4.63   At the end of the policy period it is usual to talk of the policy being renewed, but in reality a new policy is taken out, as each policy is a new contract.

4.64   The practice is for insurers to write a reminder to the broker a few months before the expiry of the policy, and invite submission of a proposal form for renewal. A new proposal form will be needed, and one of the things underwriters may do is to check it against the previous year's form. If answers have changed, then it might be useful to provide an explanation. Equal care should be taken every year when completing the form. The duty of disclosure arises again on renewal, in exactly the same way as when the first proposal form is completed (see paragraph 4.41–4.49).

4.65   It will help the architect if he ensures that the new proposal form is sent to his broker at least four weeks before the expiry of the existing policy. This could save the architect money as well as trouble, as it is important to give the broker time to negotiate good terms.

Changing insurers

4.66   Problems can arise if the architect changes his insurers. A short term saving in premium could prove costly in the long term. If a difference arises, insurers are more likely to give the benefit of the doubt to an architect who has been with them for some time than to one who has only recently become insured with them. Insurers do not favour the architect who is forever moving his business. For example, say that a claim is notified under the 1995 policy but arguably should have been notified under under the 1993 policy. If the current insurers were also on risk in 1993 they may agree to accept the claim since they would have had to cover it anyway. This would not apply if different insurers were involved in 1993.

4.67   Even if he is careful, the architect can find that a claim is not covered by either his old or new insurers. On renewal, great care always needs to be taken to ensure that any circumstances which could give rise to a claim are notified before the expiry of the old policy, and this is especially the case if the architect is changing insurers. Any claim arising from circumstances notified to previous insurers will be covered by the old policy, as will developments of a claim previously notified. What may be difficult to determine is whether a claim does arise from circumstances, or is a development of a claim, previously notified or not.

4.68   This is illustrated by a case decided by the Court of Appeal in 1987, *Thorman v New Hampshire Insurance Co (UK) Ltd* 39 BLR 41. In May 1973 the plaintiff architect was engaged to design and inspect the construction of a housing development in Exeter. Following completion, various defects became apparent which the client building owners alleged were due to the architect's negligence. In particular, there had been a history of problems with the brickwork, and in May 1982 the client's solicitors wrote to the architect referring in general terms to problems that had arisen. The architect notified his insurers, New Hampshire, of a claim. In October 1983 he changed insurers, and thereafter was covered by the Home Insurance. Despite requests for details of the allegations from the client's solicitors, none were forthcoming until the statement of claim was served in 1984, that is after the architect had changed insurers. At that time, it became clear that more than the brickwork was involved and there were further defects.

4.69   The question was whether New Hampshire were under an obligation to indemnify the architect in respect of the various other matters as well as defects with the brickwork or whether the Home were obliged to indemnify him in respect of the other matters. Were the other matters part of the claim notified in 1982, or did they constitute a new claim to be dealt with under the new policy? On the facts, the court decided the former and that New Hampshire were the insurers in respect of all the complaints. However, the architect had to go to the Court of Appeal to establish this.

4.70   Another example of the problems that can arise when changing insurers is *BNP v Page and Wells,* see paragraphs 7.09–7.10.

4.71   An additional problem is that the new insurers may, by endorsement, exclude from cover claims arising on named projects where circumstances or claims have been notified to previous insurers. In that case it is clear that the practice will not have cover for new claims, although there is still the problem of establishing what constitutes a new claim.

5   The policy wording

5.01   This section looks at the policy wording, which may be a printed or typed document and is often referred to as the *policy*. In this book, it is called the policy wording, or wording, as the policy (the contract between the insured and insurers) comprises a number of documents, as explained in paragraph 3.02. There is no standard form of wording for architects' professional indemnity insurance, although the various wordings used have largely similar features.

The insuring clauses

5.02   The insuring clauses state the indemnity that insurers agree to give. Architects' professional indemnity policies do not all give the same breadth of cover. The wordings currently to be found on the market, for architects and other construction design professionals, can be divided into three categories, giving cover for claims arising out of

- negligence;
- breach of professional duty;
- civil liability.

5.03   Examples of negligence wording are: *We, the insurers, hereby agree to indemnify the Insured for any sum which the Insured becomes legally liable to pay arising from any claim as a direct result of any negligent act, error or omission,* or sometimes *negligent act, negligent error or negligent omission* (whether there is any practical difference between these is a moot point) or *any negligence whether by act, error or omission.*

5.04   An example of breach of professional duty wording is: *The Insured is indemnified against any claim for which the Insured shall become legally liable to pay in consequence of any breach of the professional duty of care owed by the Insured to the claimant.* Although the reference to breach of the professional duty of care seems to suggest liability in the tort of negligence, what is covered is damages resulting from a breach of the architect's liability as a professional man. Such liability may be in contract, tort or under statute and may be wider than negligence. Wordings such as *breach of professional duty resulting in negligent act, error or omission* may be found or *breach of duty by reason of any neglect, omission or error.* Since the breach is linked to negligence, these are negligence wordings.

5.05 An example of civil liability wording is *any legal liability or alleged legal liability.* Cover for breach of professional duty is wider than that for negligence, and civil liability wording is wider still. It is necessary though to consider all the terms of the wording, in particular the exclusions and conditions, when assessing the extent of cover. Some architects' wordings are for negligence only and some for breach of professional duty. Civil liability wording is not uncommon for engineers, but is not usually available for architects.

5.06 The wording will limit cover to claims arising as a result of negligence or breach of duty *in the professional conduct of the Insured's business* or *in the exercise or conduct of the Insured's professional business.* An architect will owe duties to his employees and to third parties (for example with regard to the safety of his premises, or the way he drives his car) but a breach of those duties is not a breach in the conduct of his professional business. If one of his staff is injured in the office, or he has an accident on his way to a site meeting, the architect should have insurance cover for those risks, but it will not be under his professional indemnity policy. Activities which are not normally part of an architect's professional business will also not usually be covered, unless the policy is extended. Examples are planning supervision (see paragraphs 6.38–6.44) and project management (see paragraph 6.37).

5.07 Some policy wordings expressly state that claims arising from breach of warranty of authority are included within the cover, although depending upon the wording, such claims would arguably be covered in any event.

5.08 To what extent are higher obligations, such as those found in non-standard conditions of engagement and collateral warranties, covered? Professional negligence is breach of the obligation to exercise reasonable skill and care in accordance with the standards of the reasonably competent professional person. What about a requirement that the architect exercise *the standard of skill and care to be expected of a properly qualified and competent architect experienced in carrying out projects of a similar size, scope and complexity to the development?* This wording increases the standard required, albeit marginally, from that of a reasonably competent to an experienced architect. In the case of breach of duty wording, there would be cover. Whether there would be cover under a negligence wording is not entirely clear, although it would be a hard insurer who would quibble.

FITNESS FOR PURPOSE OBLIGATIONS

5.09   The standard of care normally expected of a professional person is that of reasonable skill and care. Fitness for purpose is a higher obligation, because it is an absolute requirement to achieve a certain result. If the result is not achieved, the architect is liable regardless of fault. One example of the difference is that if the obligation is to take reasonable skill and care, it is a defence to demonstrate that the architect acted in accordance with 'the state of the art' at the time. In the case of a fitness for purpose obligation, this is not a defence.

5.10   Are claims arising out of a fitness for purpose obligation covered? The answer will depend upon the policy wording but generally, no. In the case of negligence wording, clearly they are not. On the other hand, in the case of breach of duty wording, they might be. All the terms of the policy must be considered, in particular the exclusions. For example an exclusion of *any claims arising out of performance warranties* would probably exclude claims based on a fitness for purpose obligation (see also paragraph 5.45). An exclusion such as the following makes the position clear: *This Policy shall not indemnify the Insured in respect of claims arising from the giving by the Insured of any express guarantee (including without limitation any express warranty of fitness of purpose).* It would therefore be as well for the architect to avoid signing any conditions of engagement or collateral warranties which impose fitness for purpose obligations.

5.11   Assuming that a claim arising out of a fitness for purpose obligation is not covered, there might be cover in so far as the claim results from the architect's negligence. For example the exclusions above may be qualified by words such as *save that this shall not apply to liability which would have attached to the Insured in the absence of such an express warranty or guarantee.* This might lead to the curious situation where it suited the architect to argue that he was negligent.

INDEMNITIES

5.12 An example of an indemnity is: *The Architect shall indemnify and hold harmless the Client against all claims, damages, losses and expenses arising from a failure by the Architect to comply with the terms of this Deed.* What is recoverable under an indemnity will depend upon the wording of the clause, but the damages may well be greater than those generally recoverable in contract, the time within which recovery can be made will usually be longer, and liability may not be dependent upon the architect being negligent.

5.13 What cover is there for claims arising from an indemnity or hold harmless clause? It will depend upon the form of the indemnity as well as the policy wording. Perhaps surprisingly, there is not always a clear answer to the question. In the case of negligence wording, there would be no cover if the indemnity is not dependent upon the architect being negligent. Also, a few wordings spell out clearly that there is no cover for indemnities. For example, the exclusion clause referred to at the end of paragraph 5.10 may also refer to *any agreement on the part of the Insured to indemnify or hold harmless any other party.*

5.14 Claims arising from some indemnities may be covered under some policies. However, insurers probably do not intend to provide cover for indemnity claims and they might well argue that they are caught by an exclusion of claims *arising out of performance warranties or guarantees which increase the Insured's liability* (see paragraph 5.45). Alternatively, they might argue that they constitute penalties, which are generally excluded (see paragraph 5.42). Since the position is unclear, it would be as well for the architect to regard indemnities as potentially uninsured and uninsurable, and make sure that he does not sign any conditions of engagement or collateral warranties which include them.

THE PREMIUM

5.15 One requirement for a valid contract (under the law of England and Wales although not Scotland) is consideration, and in the case of an insurance policy this is payment of the premium. Most policies will therefore recite that the insurers' promises to indemnify the insured are made *in consideration of the premium.* Alternatively, the recitals may refer to *the insured having paid the premium.*

5.16   Non-payment of the premium does not in itself render the policy
        void or inoperative, nor does it entitle insurers to repudiate the
        policy or liability for a claim made under it, unless non-payment
        amounts to repudiation by the insured, that is, an indication that
        he does not regard himself as bound by the terms of the contract.
        Non-payment would however entitle insurers to sue the insured for
        recovery. The wording may give insurers the express right to
        cancel the policy if the premium is not paid.

5.17   Except in the case of a small premium, it is often possible to
        arrange to pay in instalments.

Conditions

5.18   Every policy wording will have a section headed Conditions. There
        is some overlap between exclusions and conditions, with some
        matters appearing in the exclusions section in one wording and the
        conditions section in another, but discussed below are some
        provisions commonly found in the conditions section.

5.19   Conditions relating to the notification and handling of claims are
        discussed in section 7.

CONDITIONS PRECEDENT

5.20   Some or all of the conditions may be described as *conditions
        precedent to the insurers liability*. If a condition precedent is not
        fulfilled, insurers are entitled to deny liability under the policy. In
        other words, the condition being fulfilled is a prerequisite to
        insurers being liable to indemnify the insured, although they must
        take the point. An example of a condition precedent is: *The
        Insured shall as a condition precedent to its right to be indemnified
        under this policy give to Insurers as soon as possible details in
        writing of any claim against it.*

5.21   In the case of other conditions, in legal language they are terms of
        the policy and if they are not fulfilled, insurers are entitled to
        damages as a result of the breach, assuming that they can show
        that they have suffered a loss, but they are still liable to indemnify
        the insured under the policy.

SURVEYS AND VALUATIONS

5.22   If an architect or any of his colleagues or staff undertake surveys
        or valuations, it is necessary to check that the policy covers such
        work, and the architect should in any event advise his broker.
        With regard to the policy wording, it is common to find a
        condition requiring that any survey or valuation report must be in
        writing and be undertaken by a person with certain qualifications
        or experience (for example, be a qualified surveyor or architect
        and have at least one year's experience, or alternatively have at
        least five years' experience). Some policies also require that certain
        caveats or warnings be included in reports, for example regarding
        parts of the structure that are covered or inaccessible and therefore
        cannot be inspected.

SUBROGATION RIGHTS

5.23   Insurers' subrogation rights are the rights they have, once they have
        paid a claim, to step into the shoes of their insured and pursue any
        rights he has to recover the loss from others. For example, say an
        architect is engaged to undertake design work on a project and
        employs the structural engineer as his sub-consultant. If the architect
        is sued by his client in respect of an error made by the engineer, the
        architect will be liable. Once the architect's insurers have satisfied the
        client's claim, they can pursue the remedies the architect has against
        the engineer, and do this in the architect's name.

5.24   In the example above, the engineer was the architect's sub-
        consultant. If the error was made by an engineer employed in-
        house by the architect's firm, the firm would have a right to
        pursue the engineer, being the person who actually made the
        mistake (unless the engineer's contract of employment provided
        otherwise). The firm's insurers could therefore also pursue the
        employee, exercising their rights of subrogation.

5.25   It is usual therefore for insurers to waive any subrogation rights
        they have against employees, except in the case of dishonesty. A
        typical clause would read: *If any payment is made under this policy
        in respect of a claim, the Insurer shall be subrogated to all the
        Insured's rights of recovery in relation thereto. Insurers shall not
        exercise any such right against any employee or former employee of
        the Insured unless the claim has been brought about or contributed*

to by the dishonest, fraudulent, criminal or malicious act or omission of the employee or former employee.

5.26   Upon request, insurers might agree to extend the waiver of subrogation rights, for example to exclude their rights to pursue a self-employed architect engaged by the architect (see paragraph 3.30).

QC CLAUSE

5.27   Some professional indemnity policies include what is known as a QC clause, providing that disputes between the insurer and the insured shall be referred to a Queen's Counsel (or senior barrister). Typical wording is: *Any dispute of difference arising hereunder between the Insured and the Insurer shall be referred to a Queen's Counsel of the English Bar to be mutually agreed between the Insured and the Insurer or in the event of disagreement to be appointed by the Chairman of the Bar Council.*

5.28   The clause quoted above is a form of alternative dispute resolution, rather than an arbitration, clause. The difference is that the decision of an arbitrator is binding on the parties in the same way that a decision of a judge is, whereas decisions reached in the course of an alternative dispute resolution process such as mediation or conciliation (either by the parties reaching agreement or a third party making a recommendation) are not. Either party can invoke the QC clause, which is an inexpensive, straightforward and speedy way to resolve disputes. It is usual for written submissions to be sent to the Queen's Counsel, and for him to give a written opinion. If either party is not prepared to use the procedure, the other party cannot compel it to do so.

5.29   Some wordings include a provision which looks similar but which is an arbitration clause (the similarity being that the arbitrator may be a Queen's Counsel).

FRAUDULENT CLAIMS

5.30   It is common for there to be a condition stipulating that if a false or fraudulent claim is made then the policy will become void. Typical wording would be: *If the Insured shall notify any claim knowing the same to be false or fraudulent as regards the*

*amount or otherwise this policy shall become void and any claim
hereunder shall be forfeited.*

5.31   As explained, if the policy is void, then it is without legal effect
        (see paragraph 4.44). The condition applies if the insured is
        himself guilty of dishonesty, rather than if he is unwittingly the
        victim of a dishonest claim. It is also common to find an express
        exclusion of claims caused by the dishonesty of the insured (see
        paragraph 5.38).

ADDITIONAL INSURANCE

5.32   It is sometimes made a condition of the policy that the insured will
        not effect insurance in excess of the limit of indemnity without the
        consent of insurers. They are unlikely to withhold their consent,
        but they should be advised.

MAINTENANCE OF RECORDS

5.33   It is sometimes expressly provided in the policy wording that the
        insured must maintain records, which insurers may inspect, to
        support the figures provided by the insured when completing the
        proposal form, for example for gross fees, certified building
        values etc.

Exclusions

5.34   Every policy wording will include an Exclusions section, setting
        out claims expressly excluded from cover which insurers will
        therefore not pay. Exclusions may also be added by endorsement,
        if they are specific to a particular policy. Examples of matters
        which may appear as express exclusions are set out below. When
        determining whether a claim is covered by the policy or not, it is
        necessary to consider it in the context of the wording as a whole.
        As explained, some wordings are wider than others and the
        absence of an express exclusion does not necessarily mean that the
        claim will be covered.

PROPERTY AND MOTOR RISKS

5.35   An architect's professional indemnity policy is not intended to
cover those risks usually insured under his property, contents, all
risks, public liability, motor or other similar policies. Thus the
following is often excluded: *any claim arising out of the ownership,
use, occupation or leasing of property mobile or immobile by the
Insured.* What is excluded is perhaps clearer from this alternative
wording: *any claim arising out of the ownership, possession or use
by or on behalf of the Insured of any aircraft, watercraft or motor
vehicle* and *any claim arising out of any buildings, premises or land
or that part of any building leased, occupied or rented by the Insured
or any property of the Insured.*

EMPLOYERS' LIABILITY AND PERSONAL INJURY RISKS

5.36   Similarly, a professional indemnity policy is not intended to cover
risks insurable under employers' liability policies, or accident or
health policies. An exclusion similar to this will therefore generally
be found: *any claim arising out of personal injury, disease, sickness
or death of any person arising out of and in the course of their
employment by the Insured.* Claims resulting from personal injury
arising out of employment are excluded but not all personal injury
claims, for example those resulting from a third party being
injured on a building site due to the architect's negligence.

5.37   Other employment related claims may also be excluded, for
example: *any claim arising out of any dispute between the Insured
and any present or former employee or any person who has been
offered employment with the Insured.*

FRAUD AND DISHONESTY

5.38   In addition to there often being a condition regarding fraudulent
claims (see paragraph 5.30), claims arising from fraudulent or
criminal acts of the insured are usually expressly excluded. Typical
wording would be: *any claim directly or indirectly contributed to or
caused by any dishonest, fraudulent, criminal or malicious act or
omission of any partner director or principal of the Insured.* The
exclusion will generally refer to dishonest acts of the principals,

partners or directors of the insured only, but occasionally to acts of employees as well.

5.39   It is explained in paragraphs 6.14–6.17 that cover might be given for the cost of defending certain criminal prosecutions, for example under the Construction (Design and Management) Regulations 1994 (see in particular paragraph 6.15).

WORK ABROAD AND JOINT VENTURES

5.40   Some policies limit cover for work undertaken on projects situated abroad. This is discussed further in paragraphs 6.25–6.27. In most policies, claims in respect of work done as part of a joint venture or consortium are excluded, unless insurers have specifically agreed otherwise, when this will be confirmed in an endorsement. This is discussed in paragraphs 6.28–6.32.

ASSOCIATED COMPANIES ETC

5.41   The insured (either named in the policy schedule or included within the policy wording definition) may be a number of different but connected companies or partnerships. Claims made against one insured by any of its holding, subsidiary or associated companies, or by any party with whom it is in partnership, may be expressly excluded. In this case, if cover is required it would have to be agreed with insurers and confirmed in an endorsement. They might, for example, cover such claims provided they emanated from independent third parties.

FINES AND PENALTIES

5.42   A number of similar matters under this general heading may be expressly excluded, for example fines, penalties or liquidated, penal, punitive, exemplary or aggravated damages.

5.43   Fines for breach of the criminal law cannot be insured for reasons of public policy. Fines might be imposed upon an architect under legislation relating to listed buildings, building regulations or health and safety. (The cover that may be available in relation to the cost of defending such proceedings is considered in paragraph 6.14–6.17).

5.44   Although liquidated damages are not usually levied against an architect, occasionally clients seek to impose them under the terms of non-standard terms of engagement. They would not generally be covered by the architect's insurance. If liquidated damages amount to what is legally termed a penalty, they are not recoverable in law in any event. Penal, punitive, exemplary or aggravated damages are rarely claimable by litigants or awarded by the courts in the United Kingdom.

WARRANTIES

5.45   An exclusion which may cause some confusion is: *Claims arising from the giving by the Insured of any written warranty or guarantee which increases the Insured's liability but this exclusion shall not apply to liability which would have attached to the Insured in the absence of such written warranty or guarantee.* This clause would probably exclude claims arising from a fitness for purpose obligation, and a similar exclusion is considered in this context, see paragraph 5.10. The clause might also exclude claims arising under an indemnity, see paragraphs 5.13–5.14.

5.46   Could wording of this kind exclude cover for claims made under collateral warranties? It should not. A warranty is not legally the same thing as a collateral warranty. Many policy wordings which include this exclusion were drafted before it became the practice for architects to give collateral warranties, and so it was not intended to exclude claims made under them. The cover provided for collateral warranties is discussed in paragraphs 6.18–6.24.

COVER UNDER ANOTHER POLICY

5.47   Generally, there is an exclusion of claims covered by another policy, although the provision may appear in the conditions section. For example: *any claim for which the Insured is or but for the existence of this policy would be entitled to indemnity under any other insurance.* Sometimes this is qualified as follows: *except in respect of any amount which exceeds that which would have been payable under such other insurance had this policy not been affected.*

5.48   What happens if the architect has two policies, both of which
        prima facie cover the claim, but both of which contain a clause
        similar to that above? There could be problems, and the extent of
        cover might be uncertain, which is not what the architect wants if
        he is faced with a claim. If he has a policy, and is thinking of
        taking out a second one which might cover the same risk, he
        should take advice from his broker (or solicitor).

PRIOR CLAIMS AND CIRCUMSTANCES

5.49   There is often an express exclusion of claims, or claims arising out
        of circumstances arising prior to the commencement of the policy.
        An example regarding circumstances is: *any claim arising out of any
        circumstance or event which has been disclosed by the Insured to any
        insurer prior to the inception of this policy.* Once a circumstance has
        been notified under a policy, any claim arising out of that
        circumstance will be dealt with under that policy (see paragraph
        7.13). There should not therefore be a problem with cover. The
        exclusion may be wider, and not just refer to claims or
        circumstances previously notified. For example: *arising from a claim
        or from a circumstance likely to give rise to a claim which in either
        case was known to the Insured prior to the inception of the policy
        (and whether notified to previous insurers or not).* The following
        makes the exclusion even wider: *a circumstance which in the
        reasonable opinion of Insurers ought to have been known.* (The duty
        of disclosure, including the duty to disclose claims or circumstances
        likely to give rise to a claim, is considered in paragraphs 4.41–4.49;
        if the architect is in breach of this duty he will have no cover even
        if the policy does not include an express exclusion of this kind.)

INSOLVENCY

5.50   Claims arising out of the bankruptcy or insolvency of the insured are
        sometimes expressly excluded, although such claims might not be
        covered in any event, depending upon the facts. Alternatively, trading
        liability may be expressly excluded, for example: *any claim arising out
        of or in connection with any trading loss or trading liability incurred by
        any business managed by or carried out by or on behalf of the Insured.*
        The term *business* would include an architectural practice.

NUCLEAR AND WAR RISKS

5.51   A standard exclusion, seen not only in professional indemnity
        policies but in many others, is the following: *any claim arising out
        of any legal liability of whatsoever nature directly or indirectly
        caused by or contributed to by or arising from: (1) ionising
        radiations or contamination by radioactivity from any nuclear fuel or
        from any nuclear waste from the combustion of nuclear fuel (2) the
        radioactive toxic explosive or other hazardous properties of any
        explosive nuclear assembly or nuclear component thereof.*

5.52   The following exclusion of war risks is also common: *claims
        arising out of any consequence of war, invasion, acts of foreign
        enemies, hostilities (whether war be declared or not), civil war,
        rebellion, revolution, insurrection, military or usurped power.*

Duration of the policy

5.53   It has been explained that most policies run for a year. Although
        it is still the exception rather than the rule, it is becoming more
        common for policies for a longer period, perhaps two years, to be
        offered. It may be possible to buy a policy for longer than that for
        a single project.

5.54   Insurers may agree to extend a policy for a short period, a few
        days or weeks, if the architect needs to maintain cover pending the
        commencement of a new policy. However, it may not be possible
        to obtain an extension and it is always safer to assume that this
        will not be possible. The architect should therefore start thinking
        about submitting his proposal form for the new policy in good
        time, and follow up any enquiries promptly. Having said that,
        sometimes it is underwriters or the broker who cause a last minute
        rush, by themselves not doing what they should in good time.
        Peak holiday times are best avoided for the renewal date.

5.55   With the agreement of insurers, the architect may cancel the
        policy during the policy period. He may be able to get a return of
        premium calculated on a pro rata basis for the time that the
        policy was effective. This may be done, for example, by a trustee
        in bankruptcy or liquidator. A few policies include an express
        cancellation clause, which has the advantage of making the
        parties' rights clear. For example: *Either the Insurer or Insured*

may cancel this policy by sending 60 days' notice and in such event the Insured shall become entitled to a return of premium, computed on a pro rata basis.

5.56   The circumstances in which insurers can avoid (and thus terminate) the policy are discussed in paragraphs 4.41–4.49 and 7.47–7.53.

6 Policy extensions

6.01 In addition to the basic cover described in the previous sections, most policies include some extensions, examples of which are set out below. Some of these are usually offered as standard extensions to the policy and included within the premium, others may only be given upon payment of an additional premium.

Defamation

6.02 Some policy wordings give cover for claims arising out of libel and slander (and sometimes also slander of title, slander of goods or injurious falsehood). What would be insured is the damages and legal costs payable to the claimant together with defence costs and expenses.

6.03 Some wordings expressly qualify this by providing that the defamatory material must be published in the course of the architect's professional business, although this would doubtless be implied in any event. There may also be a further qualification such as the following: *provided that this policy shall not extend to any matter contained in a journal or publication or in any communication or contribution to the press, radio, television or other media intended for circulation outside the Firm.*

6.04 In other wordings, claims arising out of libel or slander are expressly excluded.

Loss of documents

6.05 The policy wording may give cover for one or both of the following: firstly, damages which the architect becomes legally liable to pay to a third person as a result of documents having been lost, destroyed or damaged, and secondly, the cost which the architect may himself incur in replacing or restoring such documents. Documents will be defined in the wording but typically include correspondence, drawings and other written or printed material but exclude bearer bonds or coupons, bank or currency notes or other negotiable paper. There may be limitations relating to computer discs and the like. If cover is required for loss of computer information, this will need to be specifically agreed.

Copyright

6.06   Two aspects of copyright need to be considered. The first is the question of claims made against the architect for breach of copyright, that is, where the claimant alleges that the architect has breached his copyright. Generally, damages payable in respect of such breaches are insured, on the basis that they are damages which the architect is legally liable to pay as a result of a negligent act, error or omission or breach of his professional duty. Whether there is cover or not would depend upon the policy wording and the reason why the architect is in breach of copyright, but no special wording is needed for there to be cover, and none would usually be found.

6.07   The second is the question of the claims made by the architect for breach of copyright, that is, where the architect alleges that someone else has breached his copyright. Costs in relation to such claims will not be insured unless the policy wording expressly affords cover. An example of such a provision is: *The Insured is indemnified for reasonable and necessary costs and expenses incurred with the prior written consent of Insurers in the prosecution of any injunction and/or proceedings for compensation arising out of infringement of any copyright vested in the insured, provided that there is no indemnity hereunder in respect of any costs that may be awarded against the Insured.*

Fee recovery

6.08   Some, although not all, insurers offer fee recovery cover, that is insurance for legal costs and expenses incurred by an architect in suing for unpaid fees. What is insured is the cost of trying to recover fees, not the fees themselves. There would be no cover either for costs awarded against the architect. Therefore if the architect sues for fees but loses the case and is ordered to pay the other side's costs, fee recovery insurance will not cover those costs – it will only cover the architect's own legal costs. Cover is only given in respect of costs incurred up to the time of obtaining judgment, not of enforcing it. An additional premium will be payable, and the cover will usually be subject to a separate excess and aggregate limit of indemnity (say £25,000).

6.09   The architect must notify insurers within the policy period that he wishes to take action, and (generally) do so before proceedings are commenced. The wording usually provides that the architect must have a good claim, for example that he can satisfy insurers that he has a prima facie chance of success in proving the basis of the fee calculation in litigation. Insurers will therefore investigate the fee claim, and may decline cover if they are not so satisfied.

6.10   Whether he has fee recovery cover or not, if the architect's claim for fees is met by a counterclaim alleging negligence (or breach of duty), that counterclaim will be covered by his insurance in the same way that it would be if the allegation was made in a claim initiated by the architect's client. Insurers will generally wish to handle the matter as they would any other claim, for example by nominating solicitors to investigate the claim and take over the conduct of the action. On the other hand, there would not be cover if the counterclaim did not allege negligence, or if there was a defence to the fee claim not involving negligence. Examples are that the client's defence was the fees were not properly payable, or were not due from the company sued.

6.11   The architect should always consider whether it is likely that a counterclaim – justified or unjustified – will be made if he commences proceedings for outstanding fees. If it is, insurers must be advised of circumstances which could give rise to a claim (see paragraph 7.07), and the architect should take no further action until he hears from them. Sometimes, the prudent course is for the architect to forgo his fees rather than risk provoking a counterclaim.

6.12   If the client has a good claim against the architect, and as a result the architect drops his fees claim, it is possible that insurers would agree to pay the fees (less the excess) on the basis that in effect they have been set off against the counterclaim. Say, for example, that an architect is owed fees of £10,000 and the client alleges that he has suffered a £15,000 loss as a result of the architect's negligence. Agreement is reached that both sides agree to drop their claim. Insurers might be persuaded to pay the architect his fees, less his excess. They might do this on the basis that if the architect sued and both sides were successful, insurers would have to pay the client £15,000 (less the excess) and the client would have to pay the architect £10,000. (In practice insurers might pay £5,000 to the client and £10,000, less the excess, to the architect.)

6.13   In 1990, the Insurance Companies (Legal Expenses Insurance) Regulations came into force, implementing the European Legal Expenses Insurance Directive 1987. The regulations do not apply, in the somewhat obscure words of the Directive, *to anything done by a person providing civil liability cover for the purpose of defending or representing the insured in an inquiry or proceedings which is at the same time done in the insurer's own interest under such cover* (regulation 3(3)). If the regulations do apply, amongst other things, they give the policyholder extensive rights to appoint his own solicitor, the intent being to avoid a possible conflict of interests. Accordingly, the RIAS scheme, for example, offers a separate legal expenses policy for assistance in collecting uncontested fees. However, perhaps because the drafting of the regulations is not entirely clear, it appears that they are not necessarily applied in practice. Some insurers have ceased offering fee recovery cover as a result.

Criminal prosecution defence costs

6.14   An architect does not expect to get into trouble with the criminal law when undertaking his professional duties. However, legislation relating to listed buildings, building regulations and health and safety prescribe criminal sanctions for breach. This includes the Health and Safety at Work etc Act 1974, under which the Construction (Design and Management) Regulations 1994 (the CDM regulations) are made. For example, under the CDM regulations, the Health and Safety Executive have the power to bring a criminal prosecution in the Magistrates or Crown Court. Fines (or, in the last resort, a term of imprisonment) can be imposed.

6.15   Professional indemnity insurance policies are not designed to provide cover in relation to criminal proceedings. Moreover, some wordings exclude claims arising out of criminal acts (or omissions), as explained in paragraph 5.38. Sometimes the exclusion clause refers to criminal acts and sometimes only dishonest, fraudulent or malicious ones. If it does mention criminal acts, it is necessary to ensure that any potential conflict between the exclusion and the additional cover referred to below is resolved.

6.16 It is not possible, in any event, to insure against the payment of fines or being sent to prison. It is, however, possible to insure against legal costs incurred in defending a criminal prosecution. A few policies have given this cover for some time, but since the coming into force of the CDM regulations on 31 March 1995, most insurers have agreed to give it and for no additional premium. The cover, which may also apply to prosecutions brought under the other legislation referred to above, will be added by endorsement, in any event until policies are reprinted.

6.17 Some insurers will only agree to pay such defence costs and expenses in cases where, in the reasonable belief of insurers, the criminal prosecution may give rise to a further claim under the policy (ie a civil claim for negligence or breach of duty). In the case of a prosecution under the CDM regulations, if someone has been injured and makes a claim or a loss has been suffered, the likelihood is that a civil claim for damages will follow, although not necessarily. Some insurers impose a separate aggregate limit on the cover (the amount may be anything from £50,000 to £250,000), and impose a separate excess.

Collateral warranties

6.18 The proliferation of collateral warranties over the last ten years or so has caused some concern about insurance for claims made under them. One wording in common use specifically gives cover for any claim arising from liability assumed under a collateral warranty, subject to certain express exclusions. However, an extension to the basic cover is not usually strictly necessary.

6.19 Case law now suggests that an architect's liability to a third party could be less if he has signed a warranty than if he has not, particularly if it is in standard terms. (The term warranty is confusing because it has other legal meanings, but for convenience the term is used here to mean collateral warranty.) However, architects are still asked to give them, particularly on commercial developments. The architect will therefore need to ask his broker what cover his policy gives for warranties, and he should check each year on renewal. It is also useful to keep a full list of warranties signed, in case one is requested.

6.20   Some insurers used to require that details of all warranties entered into be sent to them, or give cover for the standard forms, requiring to see and expressly agree cover for all non-standard forms. By standard forms is meant the warranties for funders, purchasers and tenants agreed between the British Property Federation, the Royal Institute of British Architects, the Royal Incorporation of Architects in Scotland, the Royal Institution of Chartered Surveyors and the Association of Consulting Engineers. Even now insurers occasionally ask for a small, one-off additional premium before confirming cover for a non-standard warranty. Some insurers are still reluctant to cover non-standard warranties that permit assignment to more than one party (except in the case of a financier warranty). The Wren Mutual limits cover for what is known as 'economic or consequential loss' (that is costs other than the reasonable costs of repairing defects), although the cover given is now wider than it used to be. Some insurers will confirm cover, if requested, in an endorsement to the policy. If that is done, the wording of the endorsement should be looked at carefully.

6.21   On the other hand, most insurers have relaxed their attitude in recent years, and it is now not uncommon for there to be full cover for warranties in the same way as there is cover for non-standard terms of appointment. This means that the same policy terms and conditions will apply. For example, if there is no cover for fitness for purpose obligations or indemnities, this will apply to any contract entered into by the architect, whether it is a warranty or an appointment (see paragraphs 5.09–5.14).

6.22   Many brokers, and a few insurers, will offer advice in relation to the insurance implications of a non-standard warranty. Any architect asked to sign a warranty will certainly want to check with his broker what his current insurers' practice and requirements are. However, say that an architect is asked to enter into a warranty in 1995. He has heard that there may be insurance problems with some warranties and so he sends a copy to his broker, asking for confirmation that he will have full cover if he signs it. The broker may consider it himself or perhaps pass it on to insurers. The response the architect receives is that the warranty is noted *subject to policy terms and conditions*. What does this mean? If a claim is made within the same policy period, meaning that the insurers on risk have seen the warranty and raised no objection, they could hardly deny coverage merely because the claim was made under a warranty.

6.23   But what if the claim is made some years hence, when the terms
        of the policy and insurers' attitude to warranties have changed or
        the architect has gone to different insurers? The trouble is that
        because the insurance is written on a claims made basis, any claim
        will be subject to the terms of the policy current at the time the
        claim is made (see paragraphs 3.35–3.39). This makes things
        difficult for the architect, because the claim may be made many
        years hence. The best he can do is to follow any advice he
        receives at the time, and to sign warranties in the standard form,
        or as similar thereto as possible. If he is thinking of changing
        insurers, he should also check the new insurers' attitude to
        warranties. Some insurers are prepared to accept warranties
        accepted by previous insurers, on the same terms. It would
        certainly be as well to avoid fitness for purpose obligations or
        indemnities, as he may not be able to get cover for them in the
        future, even if he has it under his current policy. Onerous
        warranties have commercial as well as insurance implications.

6.24   If a non-standard warranty (or a contract of appointment for that
        matter) contains an insurance clause, the architect must be sure
        that he can comply with it (see paragraphs 1.09–1.16) This means
        that he will have a good reason for seeking to delete onerous
        provisions such as fitness for purpose obligations or indemnities.
        Some clauses require the architect to acknowledge that he has
        insurers' approval to enter into the warranty, for example: *We
        confirm that we will maintain professional indemnity insurance as
        required by the terms of the appointment and that we have disclosed
        to and received the approval of our insurers to this deed.*
        Commercial insurers (as opposed to the Wren Mutual) will not
        give their 'approval', and in any event such a provision suggests a
        misunderstanding of how claims made policies work.

Work undertaken on projects abroad

6.25   If an architect undertakes work on projects situated outside the
        United Kingdom he will need to consider whether he is covered by
        his policy, and this applies whether or not the design work is done
        within the United Kingdom. Three matters have to be considered,
        as they are not necessarily the same: the location of the project, the
        appropriate law, and the jurisdiction. The law and jurisdiction
        applicable to a contract are usually, but not invariably, the same.

6.26   Some policies only cover work on projects situated within the United Kingdom (ie England, Wales, Scotland, Northern Ireland, the Isle of Man and the Channel Islands). It is though more usual for a policy taken out in the United Kingdom to cover all work done except that which has a North American element. Therefore work done anywhere in the United States of America or Canada, or where the applicable law or jurisdiction is that or the United States of America or Canada, will be excluded.

6.27   It would always be as well for an architect to inform his broker if he is intending to undertake work in connection with a project abroad. This does not only apply at renewal when prompted by a question in the proposal form (see paragraph 4.26), but during the life of the policy as well. Insurers may agree to cover specific projects which would otherwise be excluded, with or without an additional premium, and if so this will usually be set out in an endorsement to the policy. The architect will also need to check the law of the country concerned, since he must ensure that he has satisfied local requirements which may require him to take out separate and additional insurance.

Joint ventures and consortia

6.28   Joint venture and consortium are not legal terms of art. There are a number of legal routes that parties intending to work together (say two firms of architects) can employ. Firstly, they could set up a joint venture company in which both firms would have shares. Secondly, they could form a joint venture partnership with the relationship between the two firms being governed by a partnership agreement. Thirdly, the two firms could agree that they will cooperate on a job, in a particular way governed by a contract between them. In addition, a working relationship between two people, or two firms, could legally be interpreted as a partnership (and therefore a joint venture) without there being any formal documentation in place.

6.29   As explained, claims arising out of work done as part of a joint venture or consortium will generally be excluded from cover unless the policy has been specifically extended to cover such claims. The proposal form may include questions about such work (see paragraph 4.27).

6.30   Whatever the legal basis and whether formal documentation is in
        place or not, any agreement between the practice and another
        party to work together or cooperate, whether on a single project
        or more generally, must be mentioned to insurers, to ensure that
        there is no misunderstanding as to whether there is cover or not.
        This should be done before the joint venture or consortium
        undertakes any work, during the life of the policy if need be.
        Indeed, it is preferable for any proposed arrangement to be
        referred to the broker before any legal agreement is entered into,
        so that any insurance issues can be resolved.

6.31   Insurers will want full details if they are to extend cover, for
        example the date of the agreement, the names of the participants,
        their professional business, the nature of the projects to be
        undertaken and each party's responsibilities. They may ask to see
        a copy of any legal agreements. Usually the cover given will be
        limited to acts of the insured architect, and will not extend to the
        liabilities of the other parties or any liability the insured has
        assumed in contract for the other parties' errors. For an
        additional premium, the architect might be able to get cover for
        his joint liability.

6.32   Insurance should also be discussed with the other members of the
        consortium or joint venture and their brokers, to ensure that all
        parties have the cover they require.

Environmental work

6.33   By environmental work is meant (quoting from one proposal
        form) *all works, contracts, consultancies, surveys, inspections,
        analysis, monitoring, assessments, audits, asset valuations, design
        and/or construction and any advice connected in any way with a
        pollution risk arising from air pollution, noise pollution, water
        pollution, waste treatment/disposal, waste management,
        contaminated land including removal of underground storage tanks,
        land fill reclamation and design, chemicals/hazardous substances,
        environmental assessments.*

6.34   Some insurers are concerned about the potentially high exposure
        of environmental work, or that involving asbestos, particularly in
        view of the sums lost by Lloyd's and other insurers resulting from
        claims in North America.

6.35   At present, usually, although not invariably, architects' professional indemnity policies do not impose any special conditions, exclusions or limits in relation to pollution risks. That position could change if the insurance market becomes concerned about the level of risk to which architects are exposed. There may be questions on the proposal form designed to ascertain whether the work that the practice undertakes is likely to result in claims relating to pollution, asbestos or other environmental risks, but often there are not.

6.36   Surveyors and engineers, on the other hand, may well find that limitations are imposed. For example, some insurers limit cover to pollution arising from sudden and unexpected events. Not infrequently, cover is only offered on an aggregate basis, inclusive of defence costs and expenses (even if otherwise the limit of indemnity is for each and every claim). Some insurers place a complete exclusion of claims arising from pollution risks, and if cover is required, it may only be given for an additional premium, again on an aggregate basis.

Project management

6.37   If the architect is to act as project manager, he must advise insurers before he commences his duties. He should mention such work in the proposal form (whether or not the form refers specifically to project management) or if need be tell insurers during the life of the policy. Some insurers will say that they regard it as something normally undertaken by an architect and covered by the policy in the usual way. Others will take a different view. If insurers agree to give cover, this may be confirmed in an endorsement to the policy. Pure financial risks may be excluded, such as claims arising from insolvency, the procurement of insurance, the giving of advice on construction costs and matters of that kind. An architect undertaking project management should also avoid becoming responsible for work undertaken by others. From a liability point of view he would be ill advised to employ the other members of the professional team, for example (see paragraphs 3.32–3.34 regarding sub-consultants). If the architect project manager does employ others as sub-consultants, he should make sure that they have insurance.

Planning supervision

6.38   In relation to the work that architects undertake as designers under the CDM regulations, there are no insurance cover problems. Every architect has to comply with them, and any claims arising out of a breach will be covered by his policy in the usual way. However, if the architect undertakes planning supervision, the insurance position is not so straightforward.

6.39   The view adopted by the RIBA and architects' insurers is that acting as planning supervisor is not clearly within an architect's normal duties. Since his policy will only cover the architect for claims arising out of the exercise of his professional business (other similar terms may be used), such work is not covered. Therefore if cover is required, the policy must be extended. An architect who is considering acting as planning supervisor must inform his broker and ensure that his insurers agree to give him cover. If he does not do this, he might find that he is not insured in the event of a claim. Other construction professionals would be advised to check the position with their brokers. Although the view of the Association of Consultant Engineers and the Royal Institution of Chartered Surveyors is that being a planning supervisor is within their members' professional business, insurers may regard it as a material fact of which they need to be advised (see paragraphs 4.41–4.49).

6.40   Insurers will generally agree to cover an architect acting as planning supervisor, subject to being satisfied that he is competent and adequately resourced. Different insurers have different requirements and the architect must check what his insurers want. So far as possible, insurers need to be sure that those they insure know what they are doing. They will generally require that the person actually doing the work is identified and will ask for confirmation of some or all of the following:

- that he is a qualified architect, engineer or surveyor (some insurers may be equally satisfied if the person concerned has sufficient experience);

- that he has previous experience of the type of project on which he will be working;

- that he has attended appropriate training courses, seminars etc;

- that he is competent;

- that the work is adequately resourced;
- that there is a separate appointment.

6.41   Cover will generally be confirmed by an endorsement to the policy. Some insurers ask that the fees earned for acting as planning supervisor are separately identified. In any event, architects are advised to obtain a separate appointment.

6.42   Once insurers have given cover on the basis of certain information, it is important that the information continues to be correct. For example, if insurers are advised that a certain person will take on the work, that person must do so. If someone else is to do it, this should be mentioned to insurers. On each renewal, the architect should tell insurers if he is undertaking planning supervision, or plans to do so, whether or not there is a specific question on the proposal form.

6.43   If the architect decides to set up a limited liability company for the purpose of undertaking planning supervision, insurers must be given the name of the new company (see paragraph 4.11). If an employee of a practice, rather than a partner or director, is to act as planning supervisor, it is necessary to ensure that the employee is covered under the policy in case he is sued personally (see paragraphs 3.27–3.31). If the architect takes on the role of planning supervisor, but sub-contracts the work, he still needs his own insurance cover, as he will be legally liable to his client. He should also make sure that the sub-consultant is insured (see paragraphs 3.32–3.34).

6.44   It is probably easier for a planning supervisor to get cover if he works in a firm of architects (or surveyors or engineers) which is already insured, although one insurance company is offering a policy specifically designed for planning supervisors. If a firm of architects also intends to offer planning supervisor services, it will usually be more expensive to buy two separate policies, because there will be a minimum premium payable. Also, if a new policy is taken out for the planning supervision work, a premium will be payable straightaway on the estimated fees for the forthcoming year. If cover is added to an existing policy, the premium will be payable the following year on the current year's income.

7 Claims

7.01 The principal reason for an architect to buy professional indemnity insurance is so that he has the backing of his insurers in the event of a claim being made against him. This section looks at claims. It has been explained that professional indemnity policies are written on a claims made basis, meaning that what are covered are claims made during the policy period (see paragraphs 3.35–3.39).

Claims and circumstances

7.02 A *claim* is defined by the Oxford English Dictionary as a demand for something as due or an assertion of a right to something. In the context of this book, it means a demand for money or services made against the architect as a result of his being negligent (or in breach of duty) or an allegation that he has been negligent. The policy wording will provide that any claim made against the architect must be promptly notified to insurers. The claim need not be in writing and it need not be justified. Many wordings also specifically provide that notice of an intention to make a claim must be similarly notified (although receipt of such notice is treated as *circumstances* in some wordings, see the paragraph below).

7.03 The policy wording will also require that matters which could become a claim must be notified to insurers. Such matters are variously described as *circumstances, events, incidents* or *occurrences which might (or may, or are likely to) give rise to a claim* or *which require or may require any step to be taken to protect the interests of the insured or insurers*. In this book, they are described as *circumstances*.

7.04 When should an architect notify his insurers of circumstances? There is no easy answer. In broad terms, notifiable circumstances arise when there is a situation which could be reasonably expected to result in a claim. One test is: has a client or third party suffered (or may they suffer) damage, financial loss or personal injury which could be said to result from the architect's breach of duty or negligence? A claim might be totally unwarranted, and all the ingredients for a claim need not yet be present.

7.05   One policy wording includes this useful definition of
        circumstances:

(a) an intimation of an intention to claim against the Insured

*(b) any known direct or indirect criticism or dispute whether
    expressed or implied relating to the performance of the Insured
    (whether justified or not) which might give rise to third party
    loss or damage*

*(c) any known direct or indirect criticism or dispute whether
    expressed or implied relating to the performance (whether
    justified or not) of a party for whom and for which the Insured
    is responsible which might give rise to third party loss or
    damage*

*(d) any awareness of the Insured of a failing or real doubt of the
    efficacy of their own performance or of the performance of a
    party for whom and for which they are responsible where such
    failing might give rise to third party loss or damage*

*(e) any awareness of the Insured that materials, goods, services or
    actions specified, designed or recommended by the Insured or by
    a party for whom and for which the Insured is responsible have
    failed to meet the standard required and which might result in
    some third party loss or damage*

which may be the subject of indemnity under this Policy.

7.06   The following are examples of situations where the architect should
        consider notifying the circumstances, if his client or a third party
        has suffered or may suffer damage, financial loss or personal injury:

• where an architect discovers that a mistake has been made in
  his office, even though no one else is aware of it;

• where another member of the team (another consultant or the
  contractor, say) alleges that the architect has made a mistake;

• where a problem arises with design work undertaken by another
  consultant, but which the architect coordinated;

• where the contractor claims that his delay is due to late receipt
  of information (not the result of changed client instructions);

• where the architect's client contacts him some time after the
  building is completed regarding a latent defect;

• where a dispute arises between other parties on the job;

- where the client makes a joke about suing the architect for a particular reason;

- where the client refuses to pay the architect's fees;

- where an accident occurs on site, and someone is injured.

7.07 These are examples only, and whether a claim may result depends on the particular situation. For example, if a client tells his architect that the reason he is refusing to pay his fees is because he is on the verge of bankruptcy, there are no notifiable circumstances. If however, the client indicates that he is thoroughly dissatisfied with the service provided by the architect, then there are. (Fee recovery is considered further in paragraphs 6.08–6.13.) Since the coming into force of the Construction (Design and Management) Regulations 1994 on 31 March 1995, the architect would be well advised to regard an accident on site as notifiable circumstances.

7.08 The architect does need to exercise judgment in deciding whether to notify his insurers of circumstances. If he is in any doubt he should consult his broker. He should also ensure that he is familiar with the particular requirements of his policy wording, since they do vary. In general terms, while insurers do not wish to be sent 'shopping lists' of all the jobs that a practice is doing, if a claim may be made at some time in the future, the circumstances should be notified. If this is not done, and a claim is made, the architect might find that he has no insurance at a time when he needs it most. If the architect encounters any difficulty, for example because insurers are not prepared to accept a notification on the basis that there are no notifiable circumstances (which can happen), he should seek his broker's advice. He should also consider obtaining legal advice.

7.09 The problems that can arise are demonstrated by a case (*BNP v Page and Wells*, unreported, September 1994) involving a firm of chartered surveyors. Their policy required that they should notify their insurers of *circumstances which might reasonably be expected to produce a claim.* When an ex-employee came under police investigation, the firm was concerned that he might have been engaged in fraudulent overvaluations. They therefore notified their insurers, and gave them a list of valuations he had undertaken over a period of time, on the basis that they could be the subject of a claim. Insurers declined to renew the practice's insurance. About ten days after the expiry of the policy, a claim was made relating to one of the listed properties. Insurers denied cover on the basis that the circumstances notified were not such as to justify a reasonable expectation of the particular claim which had now arisen. Rather, it was a 'shopping list' notification which could not be effective to put insurers on risk.

7.10   The judge rejected the insurers' argument, saying that the notification clause required written notice of circumstances which might reasonably be expected to produce a claim of some sort. The actual claim when it arose would be covered so long as it was one which arose from the circumstances notified. There was no need to identify particular cases rather than the class of cases in which a claim was likely to be produced. The notification was therefore adequate. The commercial reality was that if such claims were not to be covered by the departing insurers, the firm would have to disclose the problem to its new insurers and might have difficulty in getting cover either at all or on reasonable terms.

7.11   The case is also an example of the problems that can be encountered when changing insurers (see paragraph 4.66–4.71). In this instance, the insured surveyors did all they could to comply with the notification requirements of the policy. They had a meeting with their insurers as soon as they realised there might be a problem, they obtained legal advice and gave insurers all the information they had. The judge's sympathies were clearly with them, but they still had to sue their insurers in order to obtain cover under their policy. (It should also be noted that the decision was based on the particular wording of the notification clause.)

7.12   The duty to notify not only arises when the proposal form is completed (see paragraph 4.38), it arises throughout the life of the policy. The architect should ensure that any colleagues and staff are aware of the necessity to notify claims and circumstances and that they feel able to mention problems that arise, as they inevitably will. This applies throughout the firm and is particularly important if the practice has more than one office. Some practices find it useful to include claims as a standard agenda item for partners' or directors' meetings. Tackling a problem at an early stage can sometimes prevent it becoming a claim at all.

7.13   The policy wording will provide that once circumstances are notified under a policy, any claim which is subsequently made arising out of those circumstances will be deemed to be a claim made under that policy. Notification of circumstances therefore attaches any resulting claim to the policy current at that time and ensures that the architect has cover in the future (an example is given in paragraph 3.39).

Notification

7.14   The procedure for notifying claims or circumstances will be set out in the policy wording (generally in the Conditions section). Wordings vary, but compliance with the procedure for notifying claims is usually stated to be a condition precedent to the right to be indemnified under the policy (see paragraph 5.20). Compliance with the procedure for notifying circumstances is sometimes also stated to be a condition precedent. If a condition precedent is not complied with, insurers may decline to give cover for that claim, or a claim arising from those circumstances, even though the policy will remain in force in relation to other notifications. If the procedure is not a condition precedent, insurers' sanction for breach of the condition is less draconian; they have a right to claim damages resulting from the breach, if they can show that they have suffered any. On renewal, the architect will be asked in the proposal form whether he is aware of any circumstances, and an incorrect answer to that question would constitute non-disclosure (see paragraphs 4.41–4.49 and 7.47–7.53).

7.15   The duty to notify arises whether or not the claim is within the architect's excess. In any event, there is always the danger that the size of the claim may increase. Insurers may agree that the architect can handle a claim which is within the excess himself, particularly if the excess is sizeable. However they may argue that they are not liable to pay defence costs and expenses because the policy is not triggered. Whether they are right or not will depend upon the policy wording.

7.16   Usually the policy wording requires that notice must be in writing (and in any case it should be). To whom it should be given will be stated in the wording or the schedule. Generally notice is given to the broker, who will pass the information on to insurers. If he is in any doubt, the architect should contact his broker and seek his advice. To ensure that a notification has been properly made, the architect should ensure that he receives an acknowledgment from his broker or insurers. If a notification is sent by facsimile, it would be as well to put a copy in the post. Copies of all notifications should be kept safely, together with insurers' references.

7.17   The policy wording will require that notification of claims and circumstances be given *as soon as possible* or *as soon as reasonably practicable*, sometimes *immediately upon the architect being aware of a claim*. Notification must be made within the policy period. Particular care is therefore needed at the end of the policy period to ensure that the person who must receive the notification has received it, and in time. If a letter of complaint is received on the last day of the policy period, the architect must do something about it that day, although some wordings do allow a few days' grace after expiry, during which time claims made during the policy period can be notified.

7.18   Say that a policy expires on 31 May and new insurers come on risk on 1 June. A letter protesting angrily about the architect's services and claiming recompense from him is received on 30 May. The partner involved is on holiday and does not see the letter until 10 June. It will then be too late to advise previous insurers, and the new insurers will justifiably say that it is not for them to cover the claim.

7.19   The policy wording will also provide when notice should be given under subsidiary sections of the policy, for example in relation to claims resulting from the loss of documents or for breach of copyright.

7.20   When receiving a notification, insurers will want to know what the problem is about and be given as much background information and detail as they need to assess the situation. Information given at the outset can avoid prolonged correspondence, and the notification should include matters such as the following:

- precise details of any claim made (including copies of anything in writing);
- full details of any circumstances, and why a claim may be made;
- the type and size of the project;
- who the client is;
- the services undertaken and the terms of appointment;

- the personnel involved, eg the other consultants, contractor;

- the form of building contract;

- relevant dates, eg when the architect was appointed, practical completion, final certificate;

- whether any collateral warranties have been signed;

- details of the party who has suffered or might suffer a loss;

- the likely size of any claim (for example, the likely costs of any remedial works);

- details of what is likely to happen next (including anything expected of the architect);

- any relevant background information about the problem or the personalities involved.

7.21 The need to provide information and documents to assist in the investigation and defence of claims is a good reason for keeping files and drawings – preferably for at least 15 years after completing a job (see paragraph 3.42). Without the documents, it may not be possible to establish or prove a defence. Copies of relevant correspondence and documents should be enclosed, and it is as well not to send original documents at this stage. It is also helpful if the architect suggests a course of action if he has one in mind. If on the other hand the architect considers that he needs assistance or advice, he should say so. If further action is required within a certain time (because a response to a letter is demanded or because proceedings have been served, for example) this should be made clear. The architect should take the precaution of sticking to the facts and not making any admissions or comments which could be damaging. This is because correspondence with insurers is not necessarily privileged from production in legal proceedings, in any event if it is written prior to the commencement of proceedings.

7.22 The policy wording usually requires that the architect must not admit liability or make any admission, offer, arrangement, promise or payment in connection with any claim or circumstances without insurers' written consent. Pending hearing from insurers therefore, the architect should not try to resolve the matter. The architect should also be circumspect about what he says or puts in writing. An injudicious letter fired off in the heat of the moment could cause problems later. Preferably, he should not write to the claimant (or anyone else) about the claim without insurers' agreement.

7.23   Although the claimant may be aware that the architect has professional indemnity insurance, it is generally not in the architect's best interests to advertise the fact, as he may then just be regarded as a 'deep pocket'. A few policy wordings specifically provide that, once a claim has been made, the architect must not disclose that he has insurance.

Claims handling

7.24   The policy wording will give insurers express rights in relation to the handling of claims. Typically, insurers will be entitled, if they wish, *to take over and conduct, in the name of the insured, the investigation, settlement or defence of any claim or circumstances.* They are also generally given *full discretion in the conduct of the same.* The way in which claims are handled varies. Most insurers writing this sort of business have some in-house claims staff (with or without legal training). Alternatively, insurers may routinely employ external claims handlers, loss adjusters or solicitors to investigate, defend and settle claims.

7.25   Generally insurers will correspond with the architect through his broker, although how the matter is handled depends upon the way the particular insurers work, and the nature of the problem notified. If a solicitor is appointed, he will usually deal directly with the architect.

7.26   In order to ensure that any claim or circumstances are dealt with efficiently and effectively, the architect should cooperate fully with insurers. Many policy wordings expressly provide that the architect must give such assistance as insurers shall reasonably require. He should provide them with any information they seek. He should also keep insurers advised of developments of which he is aware, and he should do this unprompted, that is whether he receives a enquiry from insurers or not. To do so will help the architect as well as insurers, as it is in both parties' interests to resolve the matter. Undoubtedly, some problems will just go away but others will not, and careful handling can avoid a small difficulty becoming a big claim.

CLAIMS RESERVES

7.27   The claims handler will need to consider whether the architect is likely to be found liable and whether insurers are likely to have to make a payment under the policy. One reason is that insurers need to establish a *reserve*. A reserve is an amount set aside in insurers' books against claims or circumstances notified but not yet paid. Insurers must consider the proper reserve for every notification at an early stage, and keep it under review until the file is closed. Different insurers have different reserving philosophies, but in general terms, insurers must try to predict how much claims notified will ultimately cost them, although it could be years before any payment is made or the file is closed. When the policy comes up for renewal and the premium for the following year is assessed, the reserves on outstanding notifications will be taken into account by underwriters.

7.28   If an architect is likely to have to make some payment in relation to a claim or circumstances notified (for example, his excess) at some time in the future, he should consider making an appropriate provision in his accounts.

SOLICITORS

7.29   A solicitor will be instructed if proceedings are commenced, and sometimes one will be brought in at an earlier stage. When insurers instruct a solicitor to defend a claim, he will generally be acting for both insurers and the architect. Occasionally, this will lead to a conflict of interests, that is a situation where the interests of the two clients are at odds. In that case, the solicitor may not be able to go on acting for either party, as he may have knowledge of each of them which he could only have gained by acting for the other. If the interests of the architect might diverge from those of insurers (for example, because the limit of indemnity is less than the amount claimed) the architect should consider obtaining his own independent legal advice. He may in any event do this at any stage if he wants to, although he will have to pay for it himself.

7.30   Defence costs and expenses (fees incurred in employing solicitors or experts to investigate and defend the claim) are payable by insurers, subject to the limit of indemnity and excess (see paragraphs 3.17–3.21). Whether payable by the architect or insurers, however, the architect is expected to pay the VAT on such costs, so long as the claim relates to the architect's business and he is VAT registered. This is because the services are supplied, for VAT purposes, to the architect. The solicitor or expert should address the VAT invoice to the architect, who may take an input tax credit and recover the VAT. If the architect cannot recover all his input tax or is not VAT registered, the VAT is payable by insurers. This arrangement has been agreed between Customs and Excise and the insurance industry because the provision of insurance is exempt from VAT, meaning that insurers are generally unable to recover VAT they incur.

7.31   Insurers may instruct a solicitor to give them advice on a policy issue, for example whether a claim is covered under the policy. In that case, the solicitor is acting for insurers and the costs are not defence costs incurred in the investigation or defence of a claim. Insurers will therefore be liable for such costs (including the VAT) and they will not come within the terms of the policy.

7.32   If the architect does not have fee recovery cover (see paragraphs 6.08–6.13), but following receipt of a counterclaim insurers appoint a solicitor to take over the conduct of the matter, the solicitor's fees will usually be apportioned. The fees attributable to work done on the fee claim will be payable by the architect. The fees attributable to work done in defending the counterclaim will be defence costs and expenses incurred under the policy.

EXPERTS

7.33   Either the claims handler or the solicitor may instruct an independent expert. If proceedings are issued and it is alleged that the architect was negligent, it is usually necessary to call an independent architect (that is, an expert of the same discipline as the defendant) to give evidence on his behalf. Additional expert witnesses may also be required, for example, a structural engineer or quantity surveyor.

7.34   Sometimes an expert will be called in before proceedings are commenced to give advice on liability or perhaps to comment on proposed remedial works. If such works are to be carried out, it is as well for an expert to have the opportunity to see the evidence before it is destroyed. Even if photographs are taken, an expert is in a much stronger position to give evidence in court if he has seen the defects for himself. Therefore if remedial works are proposed, the architect should enquire whether insurers want to appoint an expert.

7.35   An expert has a contractual duty to those instructing him, and also a duty to the court. He will usually be engaged by insurers, not the architect himself. What he has to do will depend upon the instructions he is given, but generally insurers will want his view on whether the insured architect fell below the standard of care to be expected from a reasonably competent architect, that is, whether he was negligent. The architect may feel that if the expert criticises him, he is not 'on his side', but this is to misunderstand the expert's role and indeed his potential usefulness. The expert must be objective, and he can forewarn the architect and insurers if he thinks that a judge is likely to find the architect negligent. If that is the case, the sooner it is recognised the better. Knowing the worst, the architect and insurers can then plan how best to play their hand. When he gives evidence in court, the expert is there to assist the judge with technical issues. His evidence ought to be independent and uninfluenced by the exercise of litigation, and his opinion ought to be objective and unbiased.

7.36   Resolving construction related disputes is often not straight-forward, in the same way that planning, designing and constructing new buildings is not straightforward. If a claim results in proceedings being commenced, the litigation can be drawn out and expensive, involving a number of parties and issues. The architect is particularly vulnerable because he is often leader of the design team and administrator of the building contract. Further, if a defect occurs in a building, and the claimant establishes that he has suffered a loss recoverable in law, then in practice (though not in theory) the onus is generally on those who designed and constructed the building to show that they were not at fault. It is in the nature of legal proceedings, where much depends on oral evidence and argument, that the outcome is never certain. Insurers will want to extricate themselves at the lowest cost they can, which is generally in the architect's interests as well as theirs.

Disagreements and disputes

7.37   What happens if the architect and insurers cannot agree on how a matter should be handled, for example whether a case should be fought or not? As explained, the policy wording will generally give insurers the right to take over and conduct the investigation, defence or settlement of any claim, and give them full discretion to do so. The following qualification may however appear: *the Insured shall not be required to contest any legal proceedings unless a Queen's Counsel shall advise that such proceedings could be contested with the probability of success.* This gives the architect a measure of protection.

7.38　　A number of policies include the following provision, which adds the requirement that the architect give his consent: *Insurers agree to pay claims which may arise under the insurance without requiring the Insured to dispute any claim unless a Queen's Counsel (to be mutually agreed by the Insurers and Insured) advises that the same could be contested with a reasonable prospect of success by the Insured and the Insured consents to such claim being contested, but such consent not to be unreasonably withheld. In the event of any dispute arising between the Insurers and the Insured as to what constitutes an unreasonable refusal to contest a claim at law, the President for the time being of the professional body of which the Insured is a member shall nominate a Referee to decide this point (only) and the decision of such Referee shall be binding on both parties.*

7.39　　However, probably a more common scenario is where insurers are minded to settle a case but the architect feels that it should be contested. Unusually, the policy wording may include a provision that insurers will not settle any claim without the insured's consent. In the absence of such a clause, what can the architect do? If he feels strongly, he could write setting out his views and he may be able to talk the matter over with whoever is handling the claim. He could talk to his broker, and explain the position to him. He could also talk to a colleague or friend (for example, someone who acts as an expert), as it may be useful to discuss the matter with someone who is independent and objective. He could obtain his own legal advice, perhaps agreeing a comparatively low initial fee for a solicitor to read the papers and give a view. It is important that anyone from whom the architect seeks assistance or advice is given all the facts. The person consulted may concur with insurers' view that the case should be settled, but if they agree that the case should be fought, the architect can put further pressure on his insurers. At the end of the day however, it will generally be the insurers who make the final decision.

7.40   As a last resort, the policy wording may include an appeal procedure, for example a QC clause (see paragraphs 5.27–5.29), which the architect may be able to invoke, depending upon the nature of the disagreement.

7.41   Insurers may have the right to discharge their liability in relation to a claim by paying the limit of indemnity over to the architect, who may then fight on or try to reach a settlement. For example, there might be a clause providing that: *In the event that Insurers shall be advised by their solicitors that it is prudent to do so, Insurers shall be entitled to make a payment of the limit of indemnity (or the balance of the limit of indemnity available) to the Insured in exoneration and total discharge of any further liability in relation to a claim by the Insured under the policy.* In the event that insurers are not given this express right, an agreement may sometimes be reached between the architect and insurers that this be done (see the *Normid* case discussed in paragraph 9.02).

7.42   The architect may feel that his reputation is at stake, and that making a payment to settle a claim implies that he has been negligent. However, the economics of litigation mean that not infrequently cases are settled for their nuisance value and this does not necessarily imply that the architect has been negligent. Whatever damage – financial or otherwise – results from a settlement, the damage will be far greater if the case is fought and lost in court. A confidentiality clause could be put into the settlement agreement, although in practice it may not be possible to enforce it; it is not clear what the sanction would be and in any event once the clause has been breached, the harm has been done.

7.43   Insurers are sometimes criticised for the way that they deal with claims, in particular their apparent readiness to deny cover. When receiving a notification, the first thing that the claims handler has to do is ascertain whether or not any claim is covered by the policy. There are situations where clearly this is not the case. For example, the information given to insurers may be about a claim made against a party not covered by the policy, or in relation to a risk that is not covered. In such a situation, the claims handler is only doing his job if he decides that there is no cover. There are situations where more information is required to decide whether there is cover or not. For example, if an architect sends his insurers, without any explanation, a writ that he has just received through the post, the claims handler must ask for details of when the architect first became aware of the problem. The writ may have arrived entirely without warning, or the truth may be that the claimant has been complaining to the architect over a period of time, in which case insurers will doubtless ask why they were not told about the problem earlier.

7.44   There are situations, though, where the position is not clear-cut and the architect may feel that insurers are trying to avoid their liabilities under the policy. One way to prevent this happening is for the architect to be familiar with what is required of him and ensure that he meets his obligations under the policy. If he does not do this, he should not be surprised if he has no cover. However, situations can arise where the architect can find that he is in dispute with his insurers, and yet he has behaved properly throughout. This can happen in particular on changing insurers (see paragraphs 4.66–4.71, and the case of *BNP v Page and Wells*, referred in paragraphs 7.09–7.10, is an example of this). There may be occasions when there is nothing the architect can do.

What constitutes a single claim?

7.45   Questions can arise as to whether allegations constitute a single claim, or more than one. This is particularly the case if further allegations are made some time after a claim or circumstances are first notified. It can make a difference as to which policy applies, and whether there is one excess and limit of indemnity (assuming cover is for each and every claim) or more than one. Whether there is one claim or more than one will depend, firstly, upon the facts. For example, if an architect has a single appointment in relation to two separate houses to be built on separate sites, and the same complaint is made in relation to both houses, that might constitute one claim. Further, if the architect has a single appointment in relation to a number of houses in a development, a complaint that they suffered from a wide range of unrelated defects would again constitute a single claim. However, if the defects manifested themselves over a period of time and each gave rise to a separate complaint, they might be regarded as separate claims. Alternatively, depending upon the facts, the later complaints could be regarded as enlargements of the original claim that the architect had been professionally negligent (see the *Thorman* case, discussed in paragraph 4.68). The question arose in a case involving reinsurance policies and the Lloyd's litigation,

Caudle v Sharp unreported, April 1995. It was argued that an underwriter's negligence in writing 32 separate contracts was one claim, being a 'series of losses arising out of one event' (the event being his failure to research adequately the problems posed by asbestos-related exposure). However, the argument failed and the Court of Appeal decided that there were 32 different claims.

7.46 It is also necessary to consider the policy wording. This may for example provide that *all claims or series of claims made against the insured and arising from the same originating cause shall be regarded as one claim for the purpose of the limit of indemnity and excess under the policy*. Applying such a provision in practice is sometimes far from straightforward, as *Caudle v Sharp* indicates.

Non-disclosure and misrepresentation

7.47 Situations arise where there is no cover for a claim although the policy remains in place. For example, if the policy wording states that it is a condition precedent that claims are notified promptly and the condition is not met, insurers may repudiate liability on any claim not notified in good time, but otherwise the policy continues to be valid (see paragraph 7.14). In other situations, the whole policy may be avoided as if it had never existed (see paragraph 4.44). Avoidance arises in the context of non-disclosure and misrepresentation.

7.48 The insured's duty to disclose material facts and not to misrepresent the facts when applying for insurance is discussed in paragraphs 4.41–4.48. It was explained that the House of Lords case, *Pan Atlantic*, apparently changed the law insofar as insurers are now only able to avoid the policy if the non-disclosure or misrepresentation induced the making of the policy.

7.49 If facts that could result in their repudiating a claim or avoiding a policy come to insurers' notice, they may decide after investigation to waive their rights and overlook any breach by the architect. Pending completion of their enquiries, they may inform the architect that they expressly reserve their rights, in order that they do not waive them inadvertently. In the event that insurers do this, the architect should take advice from his broker, and consider obtaining legal advice.

INNOCENT NON-DISCLOSURE

7.50   The harsh application of the law explained above may be modified
by the terms of the policy wording. Some architects' professional
indemnity policies contain (either in the policy wording or sometimes
added by endorsement) what is known as an innocent non-disclosure
clause. Insurers agree that they will not exercise their right to avoid
the policy or to refuse indemnity to the architect as a result of non-
disclosure, misrepresentation, late notice or breach of other policy
conditions provided that the architect can establish to insurers'
satisfaction that the alleged non-disclosure, misrepresentation, late
notice or breach was (to quote from a typical wording) *innocent and
free of any fraudulent conduct or intent to deceive.* The onus is
therefore on the architect to satisfy insurers of his innocence.

7.51   Such a clause will not only apply where there is non-disclosure of
a claim or circumstance but where there has been any other misrepresentation or breach of policy conditions. However, depending
upon how it is worded, the clause may not protect the architect in
the event that he has changed insurers. This is because it may not
apply to matters which should have been disclosed prior to his
first coming on risk with his new insurers.

7.52   In the event that insurers are satisfied, a number of further
provisions may apply. For example, if a claim or circumstances
should have been notified under an earlier policy under which the
cover is more restricted, insurers' liability is limited to that
available under the earlier policy; and if the handling or settlement
of a claim has been prejudiced, insurers' liability is limited to the
amount which would have been payable by them in the absence of
such prejudice.

7.53   As an alternative to an innocent non-disclosure clause, the
following provision may appear in the policy wording, which gives
insurers the right to elect to exclude a claim rather than avoid the
policy. This means that the policy remains in full force so far as
all other notifications are concerned. *Should matters arise which
would entitle Insurers to avoid liability under this policy by reason of
any misrepresentation, misstatement or non-disclosure Insurers may
at their sole discretion as an alternative to avoiding this policy give
notice in writing to the Insured that the cover afforded hereunder
shall continue in full force and effect save that there shall be
excluded from the indemnity afforded hereunder any claim which has*

arisen or which may arise which is related to matters involving such mis-representation, misstatement or non-disclosure.

7.54   Even if the architect has a policy which includes an innocent non-disclosure clause in the wording, he must not rely on it; he must still be vigilant in disclosing all material facts, claims and circumstances and in complying with the terms of the policy.

8   Latent defects insurance

8.01   This section is about a different kind of insurance, latent defects insurance. Traditionally, in the United Kingdom, building owners have not been able to take out insurance against latent building defects. Fire and commercial all risk policies specifically exclude damage resulting from latent defects in design, workmanship or materials. Without insurance, building owners' only rights of recovery are against those who designed and built the building and are dependent upon their being at fault, and worth pursuing. The designers and contractors might themselves have insurance but that covers their liability, not the building owner's loss.

8.02   Within the last decade or so, latent defects insurance has become available to fill this gap. The policy – which is non-cancellable by insurers – can be arranged for up to twelve years from practical completion. It covers damage caused by a defect in a load bearing element or in the building envelope itself. It is purchased by the building owner to cover a particular project, and occupiers and subsequent owners of the building are also insured. It is first party insurance (ie the policyholder's own loss is covered) as distinct from third party (such as professional indemnity, which covers the policyholder's liability to another). Recovery under the policy is not dependent upon proof of fault; the insured only has to show that there is damage of a kind covered by the policy, not that there was negligence on the part of those who designed and constructed the building. Not all defects or damage are insured. The basic cover is for the cost of remedial works necessitated by an inherent defect in the structural works which causes physical damage, destruction or the threat of imminent collapse.

8.03   Although often known as latent defects insurance, it may be called a number of other things, for example inherent defects insurance or building users' insurance against latent defects. The policies now available in the United Kingdom owe their origin to those available in France to cover liabilities under the Napoleonic Code. However, decennial (in French, décennale) insurance is not the same thing. Such policies, found in civil law countries (in particular France), cover the liability of the producers of a building to put right defects within ten years of practical completion. Despite this, the latent defects insurance described in this section is sometimes called decennial insurance, because typically it runs for ten years.

The cover

8.04   A number of different policies are now on the market, and the cover varies from insurer to insurer. The following is a broad description of what is available for commercial and industrial buildings, as opposed to housing, although there is an increasing number of insurance schemes available for dwellings.

8.05   The policy period commences at practical completion, and is generally ten years, although it be may be twelve years or even longer. Sometimes the duration of the policy is less, for example, when a policy is taken out on a building completed some time before. The policy is non-cancellable for the period of the policy. It is a claims made policy, meaning that claims must be notified during the policy period.

8.06   The policy is for the benefit of the building owner and others with a financial interest in the building, such as tenants, subject usually to insurers being given notice of those with such an interest. It may be transferred, or assigned, to subsequent owners and occupiers. Generally, insurers require that they be given notice of any assignment. They may also require that the building contract, consultants' appointments and collateral warranties (if any) are similarly assigned. Some policies impose restrictions intended to prevent the insured entering into agreements which would affect insurers' subrogation rights.

8.07   As explained, not all damage to the property is insured. The basic cover is for the cost of repairing, replacing or renewing the building insured as a result of physical damage, destruction or threat of imminent collapse caused to the property by an inherent defect in the structural works.

8.08   An inherent defect is a defect in design, workmanship or materials which existed but remained undiscovered at practical completion. Structural works will be defined in the policy wording, as for example *elements essential to the stability and strength of the property or in the materials used in the construction of such elements,* or alternatively *internal and external load-bearing structures essential to the stability or strength of the building, including the foundations, columns, walls, floors and beams* together with the external walls and roof.

8.09   Inherent defects to non-structural parts of the building are not covered. However should damage occur to structural elements, any resulting damage to non-structural elements will be covered. Non-structural elements include non-load bearing walls; floor, wall and ceiling finishes; fixtures and fittings; water, electrical, gas, heating and ventilation equipment.

8.10   Some policies cover, and others can be extended to cover, defects in the weatherproofing of the building envelope and of below ground structures. Damage arising from water ingress during the first year of the policy is generally excluded and cover for water ingress from flat roofs may be limited (to five years rather than the usual ten, for example). Repair costs resulting from landslip, heave or subsidence may also be insured. Mechanical and electrical services may be covered under some policies to a limited extent, although the cover is likely to be for no longer than five years. Other policies are better designed to insure mechanical and electrical problems than latent defects policies. Cover for consequential losses (such as loss of rent, loss of profit, removal and other business disruption costs) is often available, for an additional premium.

8.11   Claims arising from the following are generally excluded: failure to complete remedial works outstanding at practical completion; damage for which the contractor is responsible during the defects liability period; structural alterations made to the premises after completion (unless done with insurers' approval); inadequate maintenance, or overloading of the premises; use of the building for a purpose other than that for which it was designed; damage due to general ageing, wear and tear; fire and special perils; wilful acts or omissions of the insured.

8.12   The policy is appropriate for sizeable commercial and industrial premises (for example, offices, hotels, shopping centres) or for large blocks of flats. The minimum premium and excess mean that the policies currently on the market are unsuitable for small developments. It may be possible to insure refurbished, reconstructed or repaired buildings where there has been renewal of structural elements, although the cover would be limited to inherent defects in the new structural works. It is sometimes possible to insure a building completed two or perhaps three years earlier, subject to a satisfactory audit check, although the policy period would usually run from practical completion, and the cover may be limited.

Technical audit

8.13   Insurers require that a checking or verification process, sometimes called a technical audit or inspection, is undertaken during the design and construction stage. This enables them to satisfy themselves that the risk is acceptable. A technical control agency or bureau acting on the insurers' behalf (usually a firm of engineers set up to undertake this work) will advise insurers on the sufficiency of the structure to be insured. They will examine the drawings and check the structural adequacy of the building, compliance with British Standards, codes of practice and matters of that kind. They undertake a sample check of the calculations and drawings; the technical auditor is not an additional member of the project team and does not duplicate their work.

8.14   On site, the agency will employ engineers to monitor the quality of materials and workmanship to ensure that the works are constructed in accordance with the drawings. They will visit the site at critical points and thereafter perhaps every couple of months. Interim reports are made and prior to practical completion the agency will send a final report to insurers, confirming that the building represents a normal risk for the purpose of latent defects insurance. If the agency discovers problems during the course of the job, they will say so at once, enabling these to be put right. If they report that there are defects at practical completion, they may issue a qualified certificate, and in that case cover is limited until the defects have been remedied.

The procedure

8.15   Usually (though not necessarily) the decision to take out a policy is taken before work begins on site. Preferably, this is done at an early stage in the design process, so that the technical control agency has plenty of time to check the design. A proposal form is submitted to insurers, specifying in some detail the nature of the development, the site, the construction, the design and construction team etc. A quotation is given by insurers, which will be subject to the certificate of approval from the agency. Insurers will issue a certificate of intention to provide insurance. The cover will not be effective until the practical completion certificate has been issued and the technical control agency has provided its certificate confirming that the work has been completed to its satisfaction.

8.16   A single premium is payable for the period of cover (although additional premiums may be payable to increase the sum insured during that period). The quotation will usually be based on the contract sum, and will be adjusted at completion to reflect the reinstatement value of the building. The limit of indemnity is on an aggregate basis but the policy may make provision for either an automatic or optional reinstatement of the limit, upon payment of an additional premium. Normally, a deposit of 10–15% is payable when work begins on site. The balance will be payable at practical completion, that is, before the policy starts to run (stage payments are sometimes agreed). There will be an excess, perhaps 1% of the sum insured.

8.17   Since the policy will be in force for a number of years, some protection against inflation is needed and this may be achieved in a number of ways. An agreed annual percentage increase may be built into the policy, and the cost included within the premium. Alternatively, the sum insured may be increased automatically each year in line with, for example, the building costs index or increased from time to time, upon request from the insured. In either case, an additional premium would be payable. The excess would normally be increased in line with the increase in the sum insured.

8.18   As well as the premium, the fee for the technical audit is required. Some insurers include the fee in the premium quoted, others do not. The total cost, including the audit fee, will be between say 1% and 3% of the construction cost. Additions over and above the basic cover will add to this figure.

Subrogation rights

8.19   Once insurers have paid a claim under the policy, they have rights of subrogation or recovery against those at fault (for example the design consultants and contractor), see paragraphs 5.23–5.26. Whether insurers seek to exercise their subrogation rights will depend upon a number of factors, including the amount involved and their chances of success. Insurers may commence proceedings against any party liable to their insured for the damages that they have paid. Those who might be sued include the architect, who might therefore find that he is pursued, not by his client but by his client's latent defects insurers (although the proceedings will be issued in the client's name).

8.20   There are two ways in which the architect can prevent this happening. The first is by becoming a joint named insured under the policy. This is not the usual route, as normally only those with a financial interest in the completed project would become a joint insured. The second is for the insurers' subrogation rights to be expressly waived. In one policy currently on the market this is a standard provision, in other policies an extra premium is payable in exchange for insurers relinquishing their rights of recovery. The extra cost could be as much as a third of the basic premium. If the main contractor is not dealt with on the same basis as the architect (by being a named co-insured or by subrogation rights being waived) the architect could find that he is sued not by his client but by the main contractor seeking a contribution from him.

Relationship with professional indemnity insurance

8.21   Latent defects insurance is not a substitute for professional indemnity insurance; even if subrogation rights against him are waived, the architect will still need the protection of his own insurance. A latent defects policy will not cover all claims that there might be against him. There might be a complaint about advice he gave in the pre-design stage, there might be defects or damage not covered by the latent defects policy, or allegations relating to his administration of the building contract, delays and cost overruns, to name but a few.

8.22   Latent defects insurance is not a substitute for collateral warranties either, although it will reduce the reliance on them. The policy does not cover all defects, and building owners will want to be able to pursue those who designed and constructed the building if they have claims in relation to defects which are not insured. It is a partial solution to the problems that a building owner faces if defects occur in his building. In the event of major structural defects he can claim under the policy and avoid the uncertainty and cost of litigation, but many other things can go wrong with a building for which there is no redress under a latent defects policy.

8.23   Will an architect's professional indemnity insurance premium be reduced if there is a latent defects policy on a large job he has recently completed? The answer is probably not, although this is a fact that the architect could draw to his insurers' attention. Firstly, unless the latent defects insurers' rights of recovery against the architect are restricted, the architect's liability is not reduced. However, even assuming that such rights are restricted, in the context of the cover afforded by a professional indemnity policy a latent defects policy on one project will not significantly reduce the architects' potential liabilities. A professional indemnity policy will cover the architect for claims made against him on every project on which he has ever worked (assuming full retroactive cover) and a latent defects policy on one project has to be looked at in this context. That is not to say that an architect should not encourage his clients to consider latent defects insurance. If such policies became the norm, and as a result claims against architects were reduced, then premiums should also be reduced.

8.24   The market for latent defects insurance is competitive and there are a number of insurers offering policies. If an architect or building owner wishes to find out what is currently available, he should talk to an insurance broker, preferably one who specialises in this type of insurance.

9 Third party rights

9.01   This final section looks at what, if any, rights a third party has. As has been explained, an architect's professional indemnity policy protects the architect, not a third party who has suffered loss as a result of the architect's negligence. The third party has no rights under the policy, which is personal to the architect, and this is the case even if the third party has a contract with the architect under which the architect is required to maintain insurance. The one exception to this is that, if the architect is insolvent, rights are afforded to third parties under the Third Party (Rights Against Insurers) Act 1930 (see paragraphs 9.05–9.10).

9.02   A third party has no right to interfere in the relationship between the architect and his insurers. The architect is therefore free to make any settlement or arrangement he likes with them. This was decided in the case of *Normid Housing Association Ltd v Ralphs* 43 BLR 18. There, the architect had insurance cover of £250,000 for any one claim. His housing association client claimed over £5 million in respect of roof defects in 350 refurbished properties in the Wolverhampton area. Having paid £150,000 into court (which was not accepted), insurers proposed to pay the balance of the £250,000 limit of indemnity to the architect, who would then be able to continue to defend the case if he wished. The housing association was, however, concerned that if the architect reached an agreement with his insurers, it would be prejudiced in the event that it stepped into the architect's shoes under the 1930 Act. This was because there was an argument as to whether the complaints constituted one claim under the policy (or policies) or more than one. If the latter, there would be more than one limit of indemnity available. The housing association therefore asked the court to restrain the architect from reaching an agreement with his insurers to pay over the limit. It was unsuccessful; the court held that it could not prevent a bona fide settlement between the architect and his insurers. The policy was the asset of the architect and he was free to do with it what he liked.

9.03   Sometimes, clauses which attempt to overcome the effect of the *Normid* decision are put into non-standard conditions of engagement or collateral warranties. The following are examples:
The Firm agrees not to make any arrangement with its insurers in respect of any insurance policy ... which limits the liability of the

insurers in relation to any actual, anticipated or potential claim hereunder. Or *The Firm shall not, once a claim against it under this deed has been notified to it, voluntarily do anything which would reduce or tend to reduce the scope of indemnity under its insurance policies or the amount of indemnity monies which would be available thereunder to indemnify the Firm were the claim against it to succeed in full.* Or ... *any sums received by the Firm from its insurers in respect of any claim by the Employer shall be held on trust for the Employer and shall not be paid out without the Employer's consent.*

9.04   Such provisions could give the architect problems in the future as they purport to prevent him from freely dealing with his own affairs. It is not, in any event, clear whether such provisions would be legally enforceable. Other similar clauses are considered in paragraphs 1.15–1.16.

Third Party (Rights Against Insurers) Act 1930

9.05   The Third Party (Rights Against Insurers) Act 1930 applies in the event that the architect goes bankrupt or, in the case of a company, a winding up or administration order is made, or a receiver appointed (and in certain other situations where the architect or company is insolvent). It protects a party, for example the architect's client, who has suffered loss as a result of an architect's negligence where the architect becomes insolvent before satisfying his liability. In that event the client can take proceedings against the architect's insurers and has the right to be paid directly by them. This prevents the insurance monies being paid to the architect's trustee in bankruptcy or liquidator, leaving the client to claim in the bankruptcy or liquidation.

9.06   Where a person is insured against liability which he may incur to third parties if he becomes bankrupt or, being a company, is wound up or a receiver is appointed (or certain other events occur) the rights that the insured has against his insurers under the policy are transferred to the third party. Following such a transfer, the insurers are under the same liability to the third party as they would have been to the insured. The Act therefore allows a third party who has a claim against an insolvent but insured individual or company to step into the insured's shoes and thus recover directly from insurers. The Act cannot, however, put the third party in any better position than the insured.

9.07   The insured's liquidator has a duty to *give at the request of any person claiming that the [insured] is under a liability to him, such information as may reasonably be required by him for the purpose of ascertaining whether any rights have been transferred to and vested in him by this Act.* The insurers come under a similar duty, if there are reasonable grounds for thinking that the third party has rights against them.

9.08   There are, however, a number of limitations on the operation of the Act, which has been criticised as a result. The first limitation is that the third party has to establish liability against the insured before he can pursue the insurers. In other words, if a client has a claim against an architectural practice trading as a company which has gone into liquidation, the client has no direct claim against the insurers until he has obtained judgment against the company. That is not to say that insurers may not make the commercial decision to investigate and defend the claim, even though judgment has not been obtained and no rights against them yet subsist. Their problem is that if their insured becomes insolvent, and a claimant knows of the existence of the policy, the claimant may decide to proceed to obtain judgment. The insolvent insured is unlikely to defend the claim, meaning that if insurers do not do so, the claimant may obtain judgment without too much difficulty. It may then be too late for insurers to do anything about it.

9.09   Secondly, until he has established liability, the third party cannot insist on getting any information or seeing any documents relevant to the insurance. He is therefore unable to find out whether there is an effective insurance policy, what its terms are or anything else. The third party may want to find out what the limit of indemnity was, whether the policy was current when he first made a claim, whether the claim was notified to insurers etc. The difficulty is that he may be loath to go to the expense of obtaining judgment unless he knows whether he is pursuing an impecunious defendant or whether he will be able to recover from insurers.

9.10   Thirdly, the Act only applies in the event of insolvency. If therefore a company has merely ceased trading, the Act is of no assistance.

Index